D1286600

IF I HAD BEEN ...

IF I HAD BEEN ...

Ten Historical Fantasies

Edited and introduced by
DANIEL SNOWMAN

Rowman and Littlefield
Totowa, New Jersey

FIRST PUBLISHED IN THE UNITED STATES 1979
BY ROWMAN AND LITTLEFIELD, TOTOWA, N.J.
COPYRIGHT © 1979 ROBSON BOOKS.

ISBN 0-8476-6136-9

Printed in Great Britain

CONTENTS

INTRODUCTION

Daniel Snowman

Speculating about the 'ifs' of history has always been an attractive pastime. Who knows what might have happened if, say, Ferdinand and Isabella had not married or if Guy Fawkes had not been discovered! How different would the world have been if Winston Churchill had been killed when he was knocked down by a car in New York in December 1932 or if Giuseppe Zangara had succeeded in his attempt to assassinate President-elect Franklin D. Roosevelt a few weeks later? Suppose that Hitler or Stalin had died in their twenties or that the Hiroshima and Nagasaki bombs had failed to go off . . . Fascinating speculations, but these are not so much the 'ifs' of history as its whims; there are no rules as to the degree of 'iffiness' permitted and the results can be as wildly fanciful as the mood dictates.*

The contributors to this volume, however, are all professional purveyors not of speculative fiction but of historical fact. In writing their chapters they were asked to evoke a strictly authentic historical setting and to recreate as accurately as possible the situation facing the personality around whom their essay revolved. There was to be no *deus ex machina*, no invented

---

*See, for instance, J. C. Squire (ed.), *If It Had Happened Otherwise* (Longman, 1932; republished by Sidgwick & Jackson, 1972.)

assassination, no melodramatic intervention of the fates to give artificial wings to the imagination. Furthermore, our authors were asked to concentrate upon a genuine moment in the past and upon the decision-making that took place at the time; speculation about what might or might not have happened subsequently was to be only a secondary consideration. Thus, the 'ifs' of this book occur within a framework carefully circumscribed by historical facts. All that is changed is that the central character of each piece is deemed to have decided upon a slightly different, but entirely plausible, course of action from that actually adopted. 'If I had been my chosen figure,' our contributors are saying in effect, 'I would and could have acted not as he actually did but in the way that I here suggest.'

The game of 'If I Had Been . . .' is one that we all play from time to time. Sometimes we pick on a character from the past, sometimes on our boss or a local political leader. 'If Only I Had Been In His Shoes' we say, with a combination of wistfulness and defiance. It's fun to imagine ourselves as other people, especially people of power and importance, doing things so much better than *they* did while not having any of the burdens and responsibilities under which they had to operate. In a more benign mood, it can also be fun—elevating even—to think of history as a parade of 'great' individuals and to try to obtain insights into its mysteries by climbing into the skins of those who seemed to preside over its major turning points. This book should serve both impulses: if you want to chide the real Gladstone or Kerensky or Allende for having been such a fool and not taking his chances, your task will be made easier by these essays; read on, too, if you want to learn something of what it was like standing at the centre of events in Russia in 1917 or Germany in 1952 or being in a position to tip the balance on the eve of the American Revolution, the Franco-Prussian War or Pearl Harbor.

So the game of 'If I Had Been . . .' can be fun, good therapy, and not a bad learning device. But it is more than that for it also touches upon a number of deeper issues that historians and philosophers have debated since earliest times. For instance, there is the question of how, or in what sense, 'I' can pretend to be someone else. We are always doing it, of course ('If I were you,' we say to our friends), but the question is not as straightforward as it may at first look. If I were literally someone else, I would be that person and not me. Thus, if I had been Harry Truman in 1945 I would have been Harry Truman and not Daniel Snowman and I would have ordered the dropping of the Hiroshima and Nagasaki bombs exactly as I did – and Daniel Snowman, being Harry Truman, would not have been around in 1978 to write these words. So: 'I' cannot pretend to have been literally and completely inside the skin and psyche of someone else. But if I am to be partially someone else, then according to what criteria do I decide in what ways to be that person and in what ways to be me? Can I put the other person into a physical setting of his period but a moral setting of my own? Which aspects of the real historical past can I legitimately alter and which not? The contributors to this volume were placed under no precise instructions in their attempts to grapple with these problems except that, in matters of personality as of setting, they were asked to alter as little as possible. Thus Franklin and Juárez and Adenauer and the rest were to be more or less the sort of people we know them to have been; if you distort history to the point of giving Alexander Dubcek the personality of Marshal Tito (or of Philip Windsor), you are back again in the land of whim.

There are two further questions of a philosophical or historiographical nature that the essays in this book may help to stimulate. The first arises out of that image of history as a parade of 'great' individuals, and the second concerns the intellectual validity of inventing historical events that did not happen or of pretending that some genuine historical events could have been otherwise.

Historians have long crossed swords over the question of

whether (and if so, to what extent) 'great men' make history. Thomas Carlyle is probably still the reigning monarch of those who like to think that they do. 'History,' he wrote, 'is at bottom the history of . . . Great Men.' Indeed, most biographers tend to imply that their chosen subjects manipulated history more than it manipulated them—if you think that Charles de Gaulle or Adolf Hitler or Winston Churchill were little more than manifestations of great social and economic forces you would be unlikely to write biographies of them. But no modern biographer is likely to go quite as far as Carlyle. In an age that has seen a new interest in social and economic history, only a fool or an incurable romantic would attribute the fundamental movements of history almost exclusively to its few leaders. Nor, except in the most academic sense, would any philosopher urge the view that every individual action—the fact, say, that Julius Caesar's mother-in-law's slave blew his nose—takes its place in the causal mix that produces all that succeeds it. On the contrary, most writers about the past recognize that the great bulk of humanity has primarily been concerned with such traditional and largely routinized pastimes as obtaining adequate food and shelter—activities that do not normally cause the more dramatic plunges and lurches of history. Nevertheless, many of history's great dramas *were* genuine turning points, quantum leaps in a new direction that had an important effect upon all that followed. And these quantum leaps, the spectacular turning points that set subsequent events off in a new direction, are invariably presided over by individuals who happen to be in positions of authority at the time.

Most of the chapters in this volume concentrate upon moments when history did seem poised to take off on one of its great periodic lurches and when there did seem to be someone in a position genuinely to influence events. Sometimes (Franco-Prussian relations in 1870, Czechoslovakia in 1968) the big lurch occurred; sometimes (Anglo-Irish relations in 1880) it didn't. But in each case it might have. What our contributors have done, therefore, is to consider ways in which the potential lurch might have been stimulated, redirected, or avoided as a result of entirely feasible action by an individual at the hub of events. So: do 'great men' make history? Several of the chapters in this book suggest that it is as often made by foolish men, or perhaps by people not fully aware of the range of action and decision available to them. Furthermore, the decisions and actions of the people at the helm might often accelerate or postpone the movements of history without profoundly altering them. For example, if Kerensky had handled Kornilov more effectively and thus prevented the Bolshevik Revolution, it is arguable that Bolshevism would sooner or later and by one means or another have taken control of Russia. Thus, these essays are not meant to imply a view one way or the other about the part played by the 'great' men of history so much as to provide data for what will surely be a continuing debate.

The 'If I Had Been . . .' formula raises a further philosophical issue. Our contributors were asked to assume that some event in the past could have been otherwise. But what *could*, and what *could not*, have been different from the way it really was? It might seem logical to think that if 'X' could have been different, then so could 'Y' and 'Z' as well. But if everything could have been different, there can be no enduring past against which to set these hypothetical deviations. Clearly, not *everything* in the past is susceptible to hypothetical alteration—certainly not everything at once, and most things probably not at all. It would be quite absurd try to imagine the whole course of French history without a Bourbon monarchy, and almost as hard to envisage the Napoleonic period without Napoleon; but it would verge on the respectable to consider (as Sir George Trevelyan once did in a celebrated essay reprinted in J. C. Squire, *op. cit.*), what might have happened if Napoleon had won the Battle of Waterloo. Thus, it might be legitimate to imagine some aspects of the past to have occurred differently—but the question arises: which aspects, and why?

This issue has been vigorously debated over the centuries and is a sub-section of the eternal debate between those who incline towards a deterministic view of the world and the advocates of free will. To an intransigent determinist, nothing in the past could but have been the way it was, while to those preferring to believe in free will, history is full of points at which alternative paths could have been followed.

Like all really interesting debates, that between the advocates of determinism and free will is inconclusive. Few serious thinkers have come down entirely on one side or the other. One reason for this is that there is a conflict between the way in which our trained *intelligence* interprets the world and the way in wich our *senses* transmit experience to us. Our intelligence tells us that there are no effects without causes, and that to the extent that anything appears to have occurred as a result of caprice this is a function of our ignorance of its prior causes. Imagine asserting that lightning or a sunset were capable of no physical or meteorological explanation, or that a war or a drop in the birth-rate 'just happened'. Such views would be greeted with scepticism for we assume that such phenomena do have causes even if we do not personally happen to know precisely what these are, and we would be disturbed if told authoritatively that this or that occurrence were, by its very nature rather than by reason of our ignorance, without causal explanation. Everything, our trained intelligence tells us, happened in the way that it did rather than in some other way in response to potentially definable prior causes. And once we are fully aware of all these prior causes, the event itself, we tend to think, could not but have occurred as and when it did.

Yet our senses transmit to us a somewhat different world, one full of genuine alternatives which can be freely resolved in any of a number of possible ways. 'Shall I go for a walk or stay at home and watch television?' we ask, confident that we are faced with a genuine choice and that we are at liberty to make a decision either way. The question 'Shall I appoint Smith or Jones to this post?' seems to fall under a similar category, and so, if you happen to be President Nixon (or President Sadat) does the question 'Shall I visit Peking (or Jerusalem) or not?' Our sense of the world is as of a universe of alternative possibilities. Not unrestricted possibilities, to be sure, but of real choices to be made, nonetheless. Thus, the way we *sense* the world, as opposed to the way we commonly *think* about it, suggests that events did not necessarily have to turn out in precisely the way that they did. The determinism v. free will debate is likely to remain inconclusive for another reason—namely, that we often adopt different methods of perceiving the *past* and the *present*. We tend to regard the past as having been a series of inter-related developments all taking their place along a vast chain of causation. The further back in time any particular event occurred, the more deeply embedded it often appears to have become in its fixed causal context. How nonsensical it would be, at this distance of time, to imagine that Caesar had not crossed the Rubicon or that William of Normandy had not launched—and carried through with success—his invasion of England in 1066. But the present does not look quite like that. As we look around us we see a world full of options to be taken, choices to be made, contingencies that may or may not arise. What actually transpires may sometimes appear to occur in response to rational considerations while other developments may appear to happen almost as a result of caprice. In the present, I sense that I am free to appoint either Smith or Jones to this post or that I am free either to stay at home and watch television or to go out for a walk. But once I have made my choice and acted upon it, it will probably not be hard for me to point to the causes of the decision that I took and, perhaps, to show that that was the decision that I was bound to make. Viewed in retrospect, indeed, many of our choices look as though they were more apparent than real, that even Nixon's decision to visit Peking or Sadat's to visit Jerusalem and, certainly, most of the lesser decisions of everyday life, were the outcome of a series of forces that were, between them, well-nigh irresistible.

Thus, in the intellectual and psychological make-up of all of us there are inclinations tugging us towards both sides of this intractable debate. One of the problems faced by the contributors to this volume, therefore, was to marry the dictates of the intelligence (by which we normally assume decisions to have been made in response to various causal pressures that are, at least in principle, identifiable) and the impressions of the senses (by which we perceive many choices to be open-ended) and to produce a plausible offspring of the two. In addition, they had to cross-fertilize the way we see the past, with everything comfortably fixed in its immutable context, and the way we see the present, with many genuine and feasible options still available. (Hence the decision taken by many of them to write of the past in the present tense.) No historian totally in thrall to a strictly deterministic view of the past would allow himself to imagine how anything in history could ever have been different from the way we know it to have been, while nobody prepared to allow himself too much imaginative leeway could be considered a serious historian. It is to be hoped that our authors have succeeded in steering a successful course between these pitfalls, and that the resulting essays help to suggest how the apparently fixed and immutable past once felt like an uncertain and option-filled present to those who helped it to unfold.

There are no doubt further historiographical issues on which some light may be thrown by a book such as this. Why, for instance, are so many apparent turning points in history political and/or military in nature? Does this reflect a bias in our own perception of the past or does it correspond to a fundamental truth? Would it have been possible in a volume like this to have included essays on, let us say, scientists or literary figures? How different would the world have been if Mark Twain had decided not to publish *Huckleberry Finn* or Einstein the Special or General Theory of Relativity? One might also ask why so many of the people who appear to have presided over history's major turning points were men. This book might have included chapters on Catherine de Medici or Indira Gandhi. One was contemplated on Joan of Arc. But the scope is not large and the reasons for this are complex.

Finally, some readers may find themselves wondering how far our authors identify with their subjects. Are all the alternative decisions attributed to historical figures in these essays necessarily 'better' (in either a moral or an instrumental sense) than those we know to have been taken in reality? It is pleasant enough to think of ways of avoiding war in the 1770s or in 1870 or of preventing one's own regime from being ousted by force in 1968 or 1973. But consider the problems of an additional dismension that would have faced somebody doing either a piece about an historical figure with a repressed streak of ruthlessness who decides to deal with a knotty situation by overt cruelty, or else an essay in which someone who historically made the 'right' decision is imagined making the 'wrong' one (e.g., President Truman allowing MacArthur to push the USA into full-scale war with China in 1951 instead of firing him). The facts of history were often pretty awful and the 'if' merchant is at liberty to suggest how things might have been better. But things might easily have been worse, and there is no reason in principle why a series of doom-laden scenarios should not have filled a book such as this. No reason in principle—except that every one of our contributors felt that an imaginary improvement upon the historical record would seem more credible than the invention of new skulduggery. Is it just that they are all such delightful chaps? Or is there something inherent to this sort of inventiveness that adds credibility to freshly-minted saints but not to newly-discovered sinners?

These questions are fascinating and endless but they are, ultimately, not the point. While this book may help to rekindle interest in a number of historiographical debates, it is not intended as evidence for or against any standpoint and, indeed, its primary object is not to contribute to philosophical debates at all. What our authors have been principally at pains to do is to interest and entertain their readers—and, perhaps, to send some of them off to the bookshelves in search of further reading about the past. If it succeeds in doing that it will have achieved its essential purpose.

EDITOR'S NOTE

Each chapter is divided into three parts. The first, *in italics*, is an explanatory introduction written by each of our authors in his own persona. The second is his invention, all or at least the bulk of it supposedly by Gladstone, Dubcek, or whoever. And the third part is, once again, by our own authors, each commenting on some of the implications of what he has invented.

If I had been . . .

THE EARL OF SHELBURNE IN 1762–5

'How I would have steered British policy in such a way as to have prevented the American Colonies from wanting to rebel a decade later.'

ROGER THOMPSON

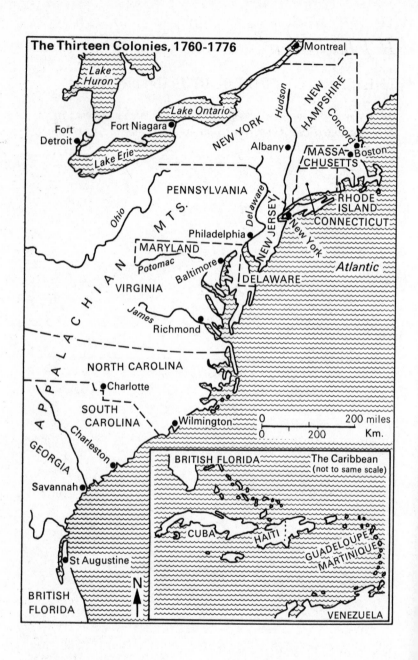

The Thirteen Colonies, 1760-1776

Montreal

Lake Huron

Lake Ontario

Fort Niagara

Fort Detroit

Lake Erie

NEW YORK

Hudson

NEW HAMPSHIRE

Concord

Albany

MASSA-CHUSETTS

Boston

RHODE ISLAND

CONNECTICUT

PENNSYLVANIA

Ohio

A P P A L A C H I A N   M T S.

Delaware

NEW JERSEY

New York

Atlantic

Philadelphia

MARYLAND

Potomac

Baltimore

DELAWARE

VIRGINIA

James

Richmond

NORTH CAROLINA

Charlotte

SOUTH CAROLINA

Wilmington

0   200 miles

0   200   Km.

Charleston

GEORGIA

Savannah

BRITISH FLORIDA

The Caribbean
(not to same scale)

CUBA

HAITI

GUADELOUPE

MARTINIQUE

St Augustine

N

BRITISH FLORIDA

VENEZUELA

1

It is a moot point when the tendency towards American revolution and independence could have been halted or diverted. Many see the period of Walpole's supremacy, the 1720s and 1730s, whose colonial policy Burke was to characterize with some accuracy as 'salutary neglect', as the time when the rot was allowed to set in. At the other extreme are those who argue that the relative calm from 1770 to 1773, with its revulsion in America against extremism, could have been a foundation for renewed transatlantic amity. Here, however, I shall be concentrating on the period from 1762 to 1765, the aftermath of seven years of war between the British and the French—war that took place throughout the colonies of both, in the Americas and in India, as well as in Europe itself. In these crucial years, certain fundamental mistakes, recognized as such by shrewd critics at the time, were committed by British Ministers.

My main problem in this exercise in hypothetical history has not been the invention of viable alternative policies, most of which were canvassed at the time, but of finding a statesman with the vision and finesse to persuade King, cabinet, Parliament and nation, and the determination to ensure efficient execution. In the roll-call of the mediocrities who formed the kaleidoscopic early Ministries of the idealistic but inexperienced young King, a suitable man is harder to find than a suitable measure.

From the point of view of office, the Earl of Egremont, Secretary of the Southern Department from October 1761 to August 1763, is the obvious candidate. Yet his concessive attitude towards the peace negotiations, compounded by his perversity in dying in 1763, disqualify him. It is inconceivable to imagine the nervy and pusillanimous Bute having the guile, drive and foresight to adopt such daring strategies. Halifax, at the Board of Trade, had the energy and expertise, but his strong suit was tightening-up procedures and fussy interventions. Creative policy-making was not his forte. This leaves us with two possible candidates for the role of saviour of the North American Empire: George Grenville and the Earl of Shelburne.

Grenville, at the Northern Department, was properly, and predictably, a hard-liner on the vexed question of the peace terms. He was, like a good accountant, methodical, thorough and pertinacious. He was not so dogmatic and pettyfogging in his attitude towards the colonies as is sometimes inferred from his disastrous insistence on the Stamp Act. Yet, however much paradox might delight the historian's mind, the transformation of a prime-mover in the destruction of Atlantic harmony into the architect of Anglo-American unity demands too great a suspension of disbelief.

Thus, we are led to Shelburne. In the autumn of 1762, he was only twenty-five years old, with only three years of parliamentary experience behind him, and not yet in office. It is asking a lot of him to expect a radical but politically acceptable approach to the problems of peace, revenue and empire. Yet if there was any man who could have averted a North American crisis it was Shelburne. His role of intermediary between Henry Fox and Bute had already blooded him in the arts of parliamentary management and the realities of political power. His ideals and discernment, however, had not been fatally afflicted. He was yet to fall under the full and emasculating influence of William Pitt. His natural inclinations tended to a liberal attitude towards the American colonies. His sympathy for dissent approved him to the New Englanders. He was already apprised of the seminal thinking of Adam Smith. Even his pragmatism, so easily and so readily interpreted as shiftiness and Jesuitism, were invaluable weapons when negotiating the ambushes and minefields of international and Imperial diplomacy.

Shelburne did not become Premier in 1763, but he might have done. Ideally he should begin his career as Secretary of State for the Southern Department, responsible for the peace negotiations with the French; then, thanks to his success in that office, ascend to the Treasury on the resignation of Bute in April 1763. As he assumes high office, we may coincidentally assume his persona, and grapple with the daunting but soluble problems of turning victorious war into profitable peace ...

In the wake of the celebrations in the United States and the commemoration in the United Kingdom of the Bicentenary of American Independence, the briefest sketch of events leading up to that event in 1776 will suffice. In 1763, after seven years of war against France, British Prime Minister George Grenville, faced with an unprecedented national debt and new commitments in North America, decided to raise a revenue from the thirteen colonies. In 1764 he introduced the Sugar, or American Duties Act, which imposed a duty on sugar from the French West Indies imported mainly into New England where there was a thriving rum-distilling industry. This caused an outcry, especially as Grenville concurrently continued the war-time tightening-up on the customs service and anti-smuggling measures. This American anguish turned to outrage when the Grenville Stamp Act, which required special stamps or stamped paper for a wide range of legal and business documents and newspapers, was passed in 1765.

Inflammatory resolutions were circulated, a special inter-colonial congress (an ominous sign of unity in a traditionally fragmented political society) had met, colonial merchants agreed on a boycott of British goods until repeal, and in many places law and order had practically broken down. Faced with the inability of the authorities in America to execute the act, a new and inexperienced Ministry headed by the Marquess of Rockingham decided on complete repeal, with a face-saving Declaratory Act which made grandiose paper claims for the Imperial sovereignty of parliament.

George III next called upon Pitt, whose reputation was still Churchillian in Britain and America, to form a Ministry. But prima donna Pitt, now Earl of Chatham, was suffering from depressive and other ailments—a contemporary less than kindly described him as a 'lunatic waving a crutch'—and was incapable of the charismatic leadership of the war years. His brilliant but impolitic Chancellor of the Exchequer, Charles Townshend, faced with budgetary difficulties in 1767, again sought revenue from the Americans, this time through duties on certain goods imported into the colonies from Britain. Predictably, colonial resistance was renewed and the British again backed down, except for the duty on tea. The Americans were not slow to learn that confrontation paid off.

The first three years of Lord North's Ministry from 1770 to 1773 were relatively quiet. The activities of the American Customs Service, it is true, led to local frictions and troops were now stationed in mobbish Boston. There was a so-called Massacre there in 1770, but despite growing unity among the colonists and a militant network of radicals intent on a breach with Britain, that particular spark failed to ignite.

It was Lord North's well-meaning attempts to bail out the ailing East India Company which did the trick. The colonists saw the Tea Act as another ruse to extract revenue from them and to exploit them to the benefit of an English monopoly. They inestimably aided a rather weak argument by turning back the tea ships, or in the case of Boston tipping 342 chests of tea into the harbour. It floated in great drifts on the water for hours. The North Ministry decided that the time had come for a little manly firmness. This reaction was a heaven-sent opportunity for American militants like Sam Adams. The other colonies united around Massachusetts in two continental congresses, and after curtain-raisers at Lexington, Concord and Bunker Hill, and the telling propaganda of Tom Paine's Common Sense, *the Americans were proclaimed rebels by King George III and declared their Independence in 1776.*

When the British failed quickly to snuff out the rebellion in America, they soon found themselves isolated in Europe. In 1781

a British army was surrounded and forced to surrender at York-
town. Lord North received the news, it was said, like a ball in the
breast, and muttered, reeling, 'Oh God, it's all over'—which it
was. In the ensuing peace the Americans gained their independent
nationhood as a republic.

2

762 Never has Britain fought a more sensationally successful
Imperial war. In America Wolfe's mortal victory at Quebec has
roused national enthusiasm. Clive has secured India. Britannia
rules the waves. Our ally Prussia has rebuffed France and
Austria in Europe. In the Caribbean, we have captured wealthy
French sugar islands like Martinique, St. Lucia and Guadeloupe,
and stand poised to capture more. Yet, despite this magnificent
roll-call of battle-honours, the Ministry faces an undoubted
war-weariness at home. The costs of conflict have been mounting
inexorably, and our national wealth is being bled away. Mr Pitt
may demand further extensions of conquest, but the price is
now unthinkable. An energetic and forceful pursuit of peace is
our first priority. I will not weary the reader with the minutiae
of the negotiating table which my Lord Bedford's despatches
from Paris catalogue. Since we are here devising a policy for
the Americas, let us concentrate on the terms we should pursue
in that theatre. In their simplest form, the choice facing us
comes down to keeping Canada *or* Guadaloupe, keeping
Louisiana, that great tract of land to the east of the River
Mississippi (which my gracious sovereign recently mistook for
the Ganges) which we will call Transappalachia, *or* Martinique.
   The popular and political pressure is strong, nay, almost
overwhelming, to retain our great territorial conquests on the
American continent, and return the islands. The war began in
Canada, and by Pitt was advertised as being about Canada.
The news of the great victory on the Heights of Abraham
signalled the turning of the tide. Unless Canada were retained,

trouble from French and Indians would be bound to cause a recrudescence of frontier conflict. A storm of protest would be inevitable at home, but more important to our policies, in America, especially New England, if Canada were tamely returned to France. Leading the protesters at home would be the West India lobby in Parliament, who would not welcome new sugar islands in the Empire to undercut their protected position.

These arguments weigh heavily with me; I would, however, adopt a less popular but subtler policy. I would let Canada go, and Martinique if I had to, and hold on to Guadaloupe and Transappalachia. My concern for the latter I shall explain in more detail in a moment; plainly I must have some vast tract of land on the North American continent to display as a sop to the public and the romantic Imperialists who are already brandishing their brushes and stirring the pink paint. But why Guadeloupe (and Martinique and any other sugar islands I can pick up)? First and foremost, because they are rich, potentially easily governed, large contributors of revenue and strategically crucial to our other West Indian islands, those 'pearls of the Empire'. Canada, by contrast, is in M Voltaire's scathing words, '*quelques arpents de neige*', acres of snow, producing little but furs and lumber, a meagre market for our manufactures with an unsettled and independent population of Roman Catholics, costly and worriesome to govern.

What of the West India lobby? Beckford and Fuller will certainly lead a vocal opposition in the Commons, but nowadays they make more noise than decisions, as they did twenty years ago. I can outgun them with the views of planters actually living in the West Indies who wish to retain our captures for security reasons. Anyway the demand for sugar and molasses at home and in North America is far greater than they can supply, as the wholesale smuggling by the New Englanders demonstrates. Other West India merchants are realizing this. Their interest is not an insuperable barrier. Even William Pitt, glorifier of Canada and friend of Beckford, is deeply worried about security in the Caribbean and will come round. Although this Achilles sulks in his tent, his influence on the Commons is still enormous.

But why provoke the Americans—smugglers, tax-evaders, treacherous traders with the enemy and slothful allies though they are? Here the shrewd advice of Bedford is compelling. He argues that the complete removal of the French threat in North America will disarm us of the last sanction we have over the colonies. The despatches of our governors and officials for the last twenty years have been fraught with the insubordination of the colonial assemblies, the partisanship of colonial courts and radicalism of popular opinion. The deterrent effect of a French presence in the St Lawrence Valley is worth battalions of troops policing Bostonians or New Yorkers.[1]

What of their outrage? Their response after the last war when Bedford handed back the fortress of Louisbourg in exchange for Madras portends a wave of fury when the whole of Canada is returned. We can of course dispense some bribery. There will be more molasses for their rum distilleries to sugar the pill. They will not even have to smuggle them as heretofore. The continuance of freer trade in the Caribbean will give them increased export markets, and earn them valuable specie, which they claim to lack. We can institute discussions with the French over a proper drawing of the northern frontier— they will be much publicized, but we can be sure that when the shouting has died down, they will collapse. We can insist at Paris on a reduced military establishment in Canada, but not too reduced. Some of my other long-term measures can be held out to the Americans as sops; yet sops will be all we need to offer while they remain strategically dependent.

I need not describe the national and ministerial relief at the successful conclusion of the peace. For weeks, the obstinacy of the French over Guadaloupe placed the negotiations in jeopardy—confirming, by the way, the wisdom of our choice. The country gentlemen in the House of Commons have predictably acquiesced in the relinquishment of Canada, swallowing the bait that this might hasten the reduction in the iniquitous level of the land tax at four shillings in the pound. As important, the King is persuaded of the wisdom of the choice on fiscal grounds. Now, as I assume the First Lordship of the Treasury, we must turn to plans for the future. The country's finances must dominate any measures of any Ministry. The national debt stands at the unprecedented figure of £130 million; interest payments alone are costing £5 million a year. No First Minister who values his place in time of peace can afford to forget the maxim of the great Walpole that he held power so long by keeping the land tax at two (not four) shillings in the pound. A policy of stringency in expenditure and finding new sources of revenue is dictated to any administration by the situation. Particular to our problem is the mounting feeling that our American Empire must bear a heavier (or at least a less nominal) burden and the pressing question of what is to be done with Transappalachia which we have acquired, and gloriously publicized.

What is probably the most contentious part of my policy deals with both of these questions, and goes a long way to solving both, at a stroke.

The Board of Trade, fortunately reduced to mere consultative status, has a humane, praiseworthy and balanced scheme for dealing with the western lands. They propose to freeze colonial settlement beyond the Appalachian mountains for the time being, to honour our treaties with the Indians, and for the future to supervise orderly and gradual expansion into the Mississippi valley. Humane, praiseworthy and balanced; I reject it out of hand.

It cannot work. How can we police a line nearly a thousand miles long to stop settlers crossing? Only with thousands of troops costing hundreds of thousands of pounds. Such a blanket restriction on migration is bound to infuriate gentlemen here and in America who have already invested capital and energy in western lands. I refer to the likes of Colonel Washington, Dr Franklin and Sir William Johnson, Americans whom it would be foolhardy to offend. The riots which are reported from various American towns,[2] supported by unemployed mobs, argue a shortage of available land on the seaboard and a need for agricultural expansion beyond the Appalachians. These are all telling points. But the crucial reason for encouraging settlement westward is financial. We have already used these lands as publicity to offset the loss of acres of snow; yet they are also the greatest real estate windfall since the Dissolution of the Monasteries. We must therefore with the utmost despatch begin the organization of colonies in the Mississippi Valley, one in the Ohio country, 'Pittsylvania' perhaps, to placate the implacable, one for southerners along the Tennessee or Cumberland rivers. For this, the name of 'Cumberland' would be a timely compliment to His Majesty's uncle.

Of course, some troops and forts and administrators will be needed in the early stages of settlement—all costing money; but the officials I shall happily see appointed will be the land-commissioners to sell the land, to speculators, so called, or to settlers, at knock-down prices (such generosity is palatable given the vast extent of the land) and the receivers to collect efficiently for the first time the nominal annual quit-rents—say 6d per acre—due to the crown. The western lands act will stipulate that all revenues from sales and rents shall remain in America, and that all officials shall be responsible gentlemen from the colonies.

Further, I propose to exercise the most impressive self-denying ordinance that any Minister in this century can perform and request His Majesty to allow colonial governors to nominate to these posts. This will reverse a dangerous trend in Imperial politics, and will arm the King's representatives with a powerful patronage weapon, which their correspondence tells us they badly, if not desperately, need.

Thus, with one imaginative and profitable policy many of the pressing dilemmas of the American colonies will be on the way to solution: a revenue for their defence and development, support from influential investors in the west, a safety valve for eastern discontents and a strengthening of the governor's political influence. No doubt Governor Bernard will now be able to buy off the troublesome James Otis and Samuel Adams with lucrative office. At home Mr Grenville and Lord Barrington will immediately welcome my proposals; Beckford will concur in time and persuade his master Pitt. The independent members will immediately see the benefit to the pockets of themselves and their fox-hunting friends.

I would not be in the responsible position I am if I did not foresee some little local difficulties. There are our savage allies. The Six Nations, the Iroquois, will not be affected; their loyalty is vital while the French remain in Canada. Other tribes to the west will be bribed or driven to conclude new treaties with us. What of the valuable fur trade, and its beneficiaries in England and America? With the French cooped up in Canada and the old Northwest ours, the Indians will come to us with their pelts.

What of the individual colony's claims to tracts of western land, claims in some cases inconveniently set out in their charters? A ticklish problem, I own, but one that careful demarcation of new settlement, the lubricant of lucrative land grants to influential objectors and the succulent carrot of office should happily unravel.

What of the fears of British merchants and manufacturers that American debtors will escape them into the wilderness or that competitors will set up industries there? But fleeing defaulters would not be deterred by a mere line on a map, and the price and shortage of mechanic labour in the new lands will inhibit the growth of factories. Provided that some of the revenues from land-sales or quit-rents are used to build turnpikes or these newfangled canals which Lord Bridgewater and Mr Brindley enthuse over, the western colonies should remain for generations a market for British manufactures and a supplier of foodstuffs for the fast-growing populations of Britain and America.

What of the expenditure in launching such a grandiose scheme, the need for communications, for land offices, for forts and military protection and surveillance, for surveys and demarcations? These will of course cost money. I might beguile the Parliament into appropriations with the promise of eventual financial freedom from the American millstone, but that is risky. Mr Grenville would no doubt propose a Sugar Act and a Stamp Act to raise the cash; Mr Townshend, too clever by half, a set of ill-judged duties on vital imports into the colonies. Here my solution would be a touch more Macchiavellian, capitalizing on the notorious gambling instincts of many of the American colonists. It is for a series of lotteries, to be organized by the colonists in the colonies. The prizes could be choice tracts of land in the west, or cash. The number of Americans who have invested in recent lotteries in this country makes me confident that tickets would be sold out on the days of issue. The profits—I avoid the traumatic word revenue—would be ample to finance the administration and development of western settlement, and would of course remain on the American continent.

My officials inform me that a snag to this otherwise foolproof project is that the Americans are increasingly concerned about a shortage of specie in the colonies. Our trade policies in the enlarged British West Indies, especially the import of Spanish bullion, will in time ease this problem for the mainland. However, if necessary, an alternative to the lottery already exists in detailed form. This is the brainchild of Mr Henry McCulloh, a London merchant with considerable interests in lands in North Carolina, and is enthusiastically favoured by that influential Pennsylvanian, Dr Franklin. Loan offices would be established in the colonies to emit British Exchequer Bills, which would serve as an additional paper currency for the cash-starved colonists and also earn a modest rate of interest, which could be used to organize western expansion in the same way as the proceeds from the lottery. The whole enterprise would, of course, be secured against the proceeds from sales of western lands. The treasury may be unhappy, but the treasury is usually persuaded by profitability and the opportunity for economics on expenditure.

There remains one vital objection that Mr Grenville and his like are bound to advance, in his case at inordinate length. They will argue that none of my plans incorporates the *principle* of the British Parliament's *right* to tax the colonies. The time, they feel, is long overdue for a sharp and uncompromising reminder that the Empire is ruled from London.

Such legalistic constitutionalism would, of course, be fatal. The Americans, perhaps the most legalistic, certainly the most litigious, group in the British Nation would regard such abstract propositions as the debating challenge of the century. They would pull out their dusty copies of Locke, *Cato's Letters, The Independent Whig*, the other old tracts of opposition paranoia and discover that they were the victims of tyranny. They would relish such laden and emotive terms as 'natural rights', 'contract', 'consent of the governed', 'justified revolution'. They might even invent some such phrase as 'No Taxation Without Representation'.

Claims to rights of taxation and parliamentary sovereignty are 'dangerous irrelevances'. Usually it is the posture of insecure administrations to hanker after the definition and exercise of their rights. True, theoretical powers of crown and parliament have been eroded thanks to the laxity of Walpole and the Pelhams. Yet, now at the end of the Great War for Empire, more than two millions of Britons in America have never been prouder to be numbered as the subjects of the young King. Mr Pitt is a popular hero there. Rather than rash assertions of rights, I prefer, like him, to adopt Matthew Prior's recommendations for treating a wife:

> '*Be to her virtues very kind*
> *Be to her faults a little blind*
> *Let all her ways be unconfined*
> *And clap your padlock on her mind.*'

This is the 'English Padlock' that will retain transatlantic family harmony, not some portentous Italianate chastity belt, which invites the attentions of every picklock in town.

This completes my policy for the immediate and pressing problem of an American revenue. Incidentally, it will felicitously help to strengthen actual royal authority in the colonies and solve some of their grievances. I see no reason why the next decade should not be remembered by history as one of unalloyed peace in America, as the last has been for war.

Though this is a novel notion at this time, I do not believe that with the solution of immediate crises my ministerial work is done, that I should now immerse myself in the congenial task of rewarding my friends with perquisites and sinecures, and punishing my enemies with dismissal and loss of favours. A Minister of this new age should transcend such opportunism and plan for the decades ahead. I should like, then, to outline a policy for the future political relations between the mother country and her adolescent children in America.

Nearly a decade ago in 1754, the Board of Trade, then somewhat more influential under Lord Halifax, devised a scheme for instilling some unity into the thirteen colonies by means of a congress which would concert certain matters of joint interest like defence. Dr Franklin was particularly warm for this plan, and I believe a fellow Pennsylvanian called Galloway was also impressed. There was even some measure of agreement from colonial delegates who met at Albany, though their provincial assemblies threw out the idea, even when the threat from the French and Indians was menacing. For which relief, much thanks! The only wise Imperial policy, as all my colleagues should have learnt at school, is that of the noble Romans, divide and rule. Any American unity will eventually be fatal to the Empire as we know it. Any intercolonial congress is bound to reveal to the colonials that they have many interests in common, and grievances too. It would be an open invitation to hot-heads and troublemakers, of which we hear there are some, to foment antagonism against Britain. Sooner or later their congress would be claiming equality with the great Parliament at Westminster and the heresy of a federated Empire —with some new-fangled title like Commonwealth—would be preached. Perhaps this must come, but later rather than sooner.

How can we divide and rule? Let me give an instance. There is concern among the mercantile classes and the treasury in Britain about the colonies issuing paper money. There are many complex objections to this, but the main one is that the notes will depreciate in value and that creditors in this country will be swindled out of their dues by being paid in paper worth far less than the face value. The main offenders are the Virginians who have genuine specie problems. The administrative response is to ban all paper currency throughout the colonies; mine, the divider and ruler, would be to deal firmly with the Virginians who have been irresponsible (a solution to their problem is anyway in sight with the loan offices) but to leave other more reliable colonies alone. My rule would be: if any measure, however praiseworthy, is likely to unite the colonies, it is *ipso facto* blameworthy. The plan for a Stamp Act in the colonies which has been gathering dust in the treasury for half a century is therefore anathema.

I have castigated the idea of any central American congress. I am more favourable to the schemes, often mooted recently, for American representation at Westminster. There are already members of Parliament like Mr Jackson and Mr Garth, and others, merchants, colonial agents in London or Americans like Mr Huske living in London, who act as an effective lobby for American interests. Mr Pitt and his followers are well known in Parliament as friends of America. Yet these are hardly proper representatives, even in the virtual sense. I am not averse to some such scheme as each of the colonies sending, say, three representatives to Westminster. I understand that even Mr Grenville, with a rare hint of imagination, feels similarly. Even better, I would welcome the counsels of some suitably wealthy and influential gentlemen from the colonies in the House of Lords. Dr Franklin, Mr Bowdoin, Colonel Washington or Mr Dickinson would be wedded for ever to the Imperial interest by such an honour; even young Mr Hancock might mend his ways at the prospect of a peerage.

Plans such as these will need careful preparation; they are not yet popular in this country or the colonies. The American members could use Lord Halifax's pacquet service, suitably adapted, to carry them in three weeks or a month across the Atlantic; American business in the houses would have to be concentrated as far as possible in each session. Forty-odd American members would not grotesquely overman the Commons and their opinions would carry great weight among the other parliamentary connexions and factions. Economically, the American members would provide effective counter-pressure against the interests of British merchants and manu-facturers. Most important, such a measure would in no way serve to unite the colonies. Transatlantic familiarity would breed Anglo-American understanding and harmony.

A last word about economics. A century ago, that great mercantilist Sir Josiah Child preached that the great object of Empire must be 'profit and power'. On this basis the whole complex organization of protected Imperial trade with its regulations, its enumerations, its prohibitions, its bounties, its guaranteed markets and its tariff barriers was painstakingly built. There are already signs that this monument to economic ingenuity is cracking and crumbling. The novel theories of Professor Adam Smith are making headway; I am myself persuaded of their merits. In the West Indies the Spanish and Dutch are experimenting with freeports. Some, at least, of the smuggling in the Americas is due to inequities in the closed mercantile system.

It would be folly to set about a radical dismantling of the system. All I suggest is a little liberal flexibility. Perhaps it would not be the end of the world if the Virginians were allowed to export a limited proportion of their tobacco direct to Europe at times of glut, or the New Englanders permitted a modest domestic iron industry. There can be little doubt that there are enormous mutual benefits to Britons here and in America from the present lines of trade. Even if the mercantile system were to disappear overnight there would be remarkably little change in the transatlantic trade pattern. What we must avoid where possible is for justified grievances to be perpetuated merely to fit the system or to satisfy the greed of interested parties.

Having thus kept the colonies in dependence, secured a

revenue, prevented American unity but fostered Anglo-American harmony, I must confess to feeling a certain modest satisfaction. Indeed I cannot find His Majesty's generous assertion of complete confidence in my Ministry altogether unmerited.

3

There we must leave our hypothetical, but not incredible, Prime Minister.[3] To ease the return to reality, here is a news bulletin:

Her Majesty Queen Elizabeth II opened a special session of the American parliament in Georgetown D.C. today. She and the Duke of Massachusetts drove from Washington Palace in the gold coach. The Queen's Troop of the Kansas Household Cavalry (The Greens) provided the outriders. Among the royal party were the Prince of Virginia, at the moment serving as a lieutenant with the Royal American Navy, Princess Anne and Captain the honourable Elmer Roosevelt. The Commons were led to the bar of the House of Lords by Mr Speaker, and Prime Minister Carter was seen chatting to Leader of the Opposition, Sir Ronald Reagan.

In the address from the throne, Her Majesty announced that the royal family had decided to take up permanent residence in America thanks to the advice of Mr Willie Hamilton. She also announced that she had raised to the peerage the ex-Prime Minister, who recently retired because of ill-health. It is understood that he proposes to adopt the style of the Earl of Watergate.

Workmen had unavailingly tried to remove graffiti sprayed on the statue of the Duke of Shelburne, architect of Anglo-American unity, outside the Houses of Parliament. The Queen was seen to smile as she read the message: 'Sam Adams Rules OK'.

NOTES

1 Powerful, though here inadmissable, corroboration of this view was supplied by Governor Thomas Hutchinson of Massachusetts. Writing to the Secretary of State for the American Colonies, Lord Dartmouth, on the eve of the Boston Tea Party, December 14, 1773, he averred: 'Before the peace I thought nothing so much to be desired as the cession of Canada. I am now convinced that if it had remained to the French none of the spirit of opposition to the mother country would have yet appeared and I think the effects of it worse than all we have to fear from the French and Indians.'

2 Not, of course, the Stamp Act riots, which would never have taken place; they were not a particularly novel form of American leisure activity in the 1760s.

3 I have not dignified this squib with notes citing sources. Those familiar with the period will recognize my debt to J. Steven Watson, *The Reign of George III* (Clarendon Press, 1960); John Norris, *Shelburne and Reform* (Macmillan/St. Martin's Press, 1963); P. D. G. Thomas, *British Politics and the Stamp Act Crisis* (Clarendon Press, 1975); Richard Pares, *War and Trade in the West Indies* (Clarendon Press, 1936); Charles Ritcheson, *British Politics and the American Revolution* (University of Oklahoma Press, 1954); L. H. Gipson, *The Coming of the Revolution* (Harper & Row, 1962).

If I had been . . .

BENJAMIN FRANKLIN IN THE EARLY 1770s

'*How I would have prevented American discontent from becoming revolution.*'

ESMOND WRIGHT

1

Benjamin Franklin is a fascinating character—or, more accurately, a fascinating collection in one physical mould, of many, often contradictory, characters. He is usually presented as one of the great Founding Fathers of the American Republic, who after seventeen years' service as a Pennsylvanian agent in London went back to Philadelphia in 1775 to lead the Revolution.* *Against this central fact in his life—he was 69 years old when he returned home in 1775—there has to be set his obvious enjoyment of the London scene and his often proclaimed wish that he might continue to live in London until he died. Was he, then, an 'Old England Man' disappointed with his British experience, or was he, as cynics hold, dedicated to the independence of the United States long before 1775? Could he, in fact, have averted that separation? What happened to him between 1770 and 1776?*

We know the facts of the world around him; about the gradual drift to war between England and the Colonies and the Declaration of Independence by the latter in 1776. But we still do not know, despite or because of five editions of Franklin's correspondence and his many letters, some of them pseudonymous, to all and sundry, what he really made of it all. Franklin himself, although he lived by his skill with words and made his whole fortune out of it, was singularly unrevealing about these crucial years, as about much else. The persona, which he developed about himself,

*For a summary of British policy leading up to the American Revolution, see pp. 15–17.

changed dramatically over the decades. He represented himself in the 1730s as the poor boy on the make—the picture of Part I of the Memoirs; *in the 1740s he was the successful printer and publisher, Mr Worldly Wiseman, for whom Puritanism brought Prosperity; in the 1750s he was man of affairs, first citizen of America, and Pennsylvania activist; in the 1760s and '70s he was colonial agent in London who was also receiving royal payment as Deputy Postmaster General of North America; in the late '70s, he was an Ambassador in Paris; and in 1787, despite his age, he was the most celebrated figure at the Constitutional Convention. There was no one single consistent image here, and his own account, his* Memoirs, *written episodically, never reached beyond 1757 anyway. He had many personae and put them on and discarded them easily, and sometimes wore two or three together.*

The letter that follows was one that he might well have written had events gone a little differently. It makes plain how a series of chance circumstances could have been handled without separation and war resulting. Franklin was at heart the least revolutionary of animals, as indeed was George Washington also. Had the American problem been handled with more delicacy and discretion by—primarily—the British government and to a lesser degree by himself, the British Empire might not have broken up in 1776. The Empire 'on this side', as Franklin called North America, would then have grown in numbers, as he forecast it would, and a British Empire straddling the Atlantic might have ensured a Roman peace in the world for the rest of history. It could have happened this way . . .

2

October 6, 1776

Dearest Child,

It was a great joy to receive your letter, to know that you had a safe and smooth journey home—even if it took 9 days' travel— and that you enjoyed your stay here. I much value your kind

invitation to stay with you, for reasons you will be able to guess
—even if we cannot perhaps now recapture the joy of our first
meeting. There is so much to say, and I am now very conscious
of all that our friendship means for each of us.

For me it is but yesterday since we took our first and precious
journey together. I still can flavour the sugar plums you made
and our parting on the shore of Block Island Sound.[1] You
were but a child and I already then an old man of 50. You sent
me in your first letter thereafter kisses in the wind, and I found
that to be the gayest wind that blows. Your favours indeed
came mixed with the snowy fleeces of a cold north-east storm
of snow and ice, as pure as your virgin innocence, white as your
lovely bosom—and as cold. I am glad now that it has warmed
to the fortunate man who is now your husband, and for whom
I predict a career of success and happiness.[2] I am even happier
that you have taken to heart my earlier advice and have
practised *addition* to your husband's estate by industry and
frugality, *subtraction* of all unnecessary expenses, *multiplication*
(which I would gladly have taught you myself but you would
not learn) and as to *division*, I say with Brother Paul, 'Let there
be no division among ye.' I much enjoyed my journey with
Ray, who is doing well in the Academy. I am glad that you
have *multiplied* so well.

I must write with caution. If you were indiscreet twenty years
ago (though for my tastes not indiscreet enough), I was then
happily married to my Debby.[3] Now I can but entertain dreams
of what might have been. I must again be cautious, or husband
William will be angry and I gather that not all your family
approve of my open expressions of admiration for you.[4] I can
only say that an old man who cannot be much longer in this
world—I have now passed the Biblical three score and ten—
must be allowed his dreams, his hopes and his indulgences.
As the good (or bad?) Duke de la Rochefoucauld says, 'Old
men are fond of giving good advice, since they are no longer
in a position to set bad examples.'

I write however to unburden my mind as well as my heart.
Your husband is now a man of affairs, and you are one of my

oldest and dearest companions. And I write in confidence, knowing that I can be trusted. For as I guard our precious memories, and I do so absolutely, so I know that you will guard my secrets.

Someone trustworthy must have my story, lest I do not get a chance to put it down in full and frankly in my *Memoirs*. I have made some mark in the public prints and my creation *Poor Richard* often carried my own adventures, appropriately disguised. But in fact I have always followed the rule, that if you want to keep a secret, keep it secret. I told part of my story in my *Memoirs* when I stayed at Twyford in 1757, but I have not since told more, and gouty as I now am, and still perished by that awful Canadian cold,[5] I now feel that somewhere I should reveal how I managed—and you will be ready to indulge an old man in his vanity—to save an Empire. I used to call the Empire a fragile thing, as fragile as a China vase.[6] But it still has much of that vase's grace, and is worth preserving.

I believe, as you know, that nothing is inevitable. Men have free will, as even my good friend Cotton Mather would admit. Life is for them to make or mar. I spent too long collecting wise saws for Poor Richard not to end up believing what he taught: but then did he not say in 1736, 'There's none deceived but he that trusts' and 'The first Mistake in Public Business, is the going into it'. I imagine that historians will see a pattern in our recent history pointing to gradual distancing between Mother and Daughter. They will even point to some pieces of mine that seemed to give it support: my faith in the capacity for growth of the New Country as expressed in my *Observations on the increase of Mankind*,[7] and my criticism of individual British Ministers. But my view in the *Observations* was Imperial, not American. Did I not also seek to extend the royal connection and to have Pennsylvania made a royal not a proprietorial colony? I was proud to hold royal office, as Deputy Postmaster General, to be a colonial officer as well as an agent for 4 colonies. I secured for my son a royal governorship,[8] and I had hopes— I can now reveal—of a colonial undersecretaryship in 1768 when the new Department for American Affairs was set up. If

Debby would have agreed to cross the sea, I doubt if I would ever have left Craven Street. The idea of separation was never on my agenda.

This is not to say that I found London an Elysium. I was proud and happy, however, to be an Old England Man. And lest my good friends in Edinburgh feel aggrieved—Adam Smith and Lord Kames, William Robertson and Sir John Pringle, Sir Alexander and Lady Dick—Scotland too. The six weeks of densest happiness I have had in my life, as I told Lord Kames, were in Scotland.[9]

If I was happy in the connection, and if—as I believe—there is no inevitability in a movement towards independence, could I have done more? In our recent testing time we must all search our souls.

Looking back, I detect three points in the recent history when I might have changed the course of history, and did not. Happily I was lucky the fourth time round. For me, for all of us, it is fourth time lucky.

First, I might well have been wrong in giving my support to the campaign in 1762–3 to retain Canada and not to exchange it with the island of Guadeloupe. At the time I had no doubts on this and wrote my own pamphlet urging the retention of Canada very strongly. It seemed to me that it would have been insulting to the Yankees to hand it back again to France, as we returned Louisburg in 1748. I thought that the West Indian nabobs in London like Sir William Beckford[10] were simply wishing to ensure a monopoly for the British sugar interest, and wanted the French island excluded for that reason. Looking back I am far from sure. My visit to Canada a few months ago taught me savagely how hostile the people there are to the cause of American independence, how grateful they are to Britain for the liberalism of the Quebec Act, and how rooted in the Catholic faith are the *habitants*. They would not have supported us had we gone to war, and they must remain a separate colony, French in language, despotic in spirit, and bitterly unsympathetic to those they scorn as Yankees.

Moreover, it seems to me to be an icy desert. I understand

that M Voltaire, whom some people call the Franklin of France, has called it just a waste of snow. The climate will forbid expansion and it will be very different in character from our own colonies, indeed perhaps before long dependent on them. I saw it as a territory into which we might expand, but I see it that way no longer. Had we returned it to the French there would, of course, have been continuous frontier war, with France backing the Indians, and continuing unrest in Western Pennsylvania and up-state New York. I wanted to end all that, but after the Shawnee War I can see no solution to the Indian problem. I think we were wrong therefore in 1763. Had I the chance, I would put that clock back. There would then have been no wild talk of separation had Canada still been French.[11]

Secondly, I think I mishandled the early negotiations in London over the future of the West. As you know, a group of us, my son William, the Wharton-Bainton group in Philadelphia, George Washington and a number of others were seeking to persuade the British government to support our plan for a fourteenth colony west of the Appalachian line. About the lands over the mountains I have a great dream. I believe there is an immense future for the lands on the Western Waters. They are fertile; the Indians are relatively few in number even though nomadic; the future there seems to me to be golden. The West will offer a refuge for the discontented and adventurous back in the Old Country; the tidewater states will look West, and there will be less readiness to quarrel with London. I once had a dream that included the hope that that colony might even carry my own name. It might still happen—who knows?[12] At any rate, when George Washington first proposed his plan for the Ohio and which—to please the Queen—we later called Vandalia, our hope was that a sympathetic British government, realizing that it could not curb settlement east of the mountains, would establish a new colony on the lines of the original tidewater settlements. All of us were buying up land, as investment and as resource for the future. I am being very frank with you in saying that some of us had hopes of a colonial governorship or of key positions in the new colony.

At times we came very close to success.

If my dream had come to fruition, all our efforts would have been concentrated on the new colony in the West, and many of the later quarrels between our tidewater merchants and the British might have been averted. The British Ministers were sympathetic, but their assistants were not. Whenever I was privileged to be allowed to meet a Minister, there was usually standing beside him John Pownall[13] or William Knox, and I know that each of them was my enemy. They took an old-fashioned mercantilist line that such colonies that were remote from the seaboard, would drive out British manufacturers to replace with their own, and would gradually produce a new economic balance. I did not myself believe that development of a fourteenth colony in the 1760s would have transformed the Empire on this side into some strange new animal, but their view triumphed and mine did not. I failed in the West. But only, as events will prove, I hope, for a while. In politics, you must be patient. And you must never give up hope.

Thirdly, and most important of all, people. Until 1770, I thought in all honesty that I was good at handling people. I had, after all, come up the hard way, and shown industry and ability. My job as a journalist and politician in Pennsylvania taught me to placate and to compromise. As Poor Richard put it, 'Full of courtesie, full of craft'. It was my own private motto about myself and the reason why I kept a lot of things secret, although I wrote voluminously in the public prints. But I came to realize in London that I lived in a different world from that of the great men of affairs. I lodged in Craven Street, but unlike the great men, I had no house in the country. I visited the Coffee Houses and I still have happy memories of my Scots friends in the Britannia Coffee House and my journalist acquaintances on the Strand and in Fleet street, but I was very rarely invited into the great houses of England. Lord Shelburne was kind, and Lord Despencer was kind, too, but then he had a reputation for being a rake, which probably hurt me.[14] I did not see the great Lord Chatham until the last few months of my stay and indeed I had called him 'The Great Inaccessible'.

Only in Scotland did I feel I was invited into private homes as a friend that could be trusted. I was immensely happy in London, but it was made plain to me that my way of life was bourgeois, my only cronies were the journalists and craftsmen, the men who had to earn a living, although some of them earned it in politics, like Edmund Burke. But until the last decisive months, I had never crossed the great divide of rank and station that marks the English way of life, and was not able to influence things where it mattered until very late. I was led to this conclusion by contrasting my own story with that of my good friend and correspondent Cadwallader Colden in New York, who was inferior to me, if I may say so, as scientist, yet became Lieutenant-Governor of a colony;[15] and, of course, Thomas Hutchinson in Boston became a royal Governor too.[16] Frankly I envied them vastly. When my son William was appointed Governor of the Jerseys in 1762 and I was myself Deputy Postmaster General, I began to hope for more from the British.

In the colonies, my reputation as an Old England Man hurt me when the Stamp Act was passed in 1765, since my friends there thought that I had been instrumental in producing it. I had, in all frankness, not anticipated the reaction there would be to it. But I thought my evidence to the House of Commons in 1766, when I spoke for American opinion and against the Act, would have set my image straight there. All that happened, however, was that the persuasiveness and effect of my House of Commons presentation, and my activity in securing the Repeal of the Stamp Act, led the kingmakers in London to see me (quite wrongly) as a rebel. The man in the middle is always the one who gets kicked. I hoped in 1768 when the Department of North American Affairs was established that I might be Undersecretary in it. Lord Grafton hinted at this possibility. Who got the job? John Pownall, the man at the desk, the crony of previous Ministers.

In my recent bout of self-analysis, I have learnt a lot about myself and others. Below the surface I saw ugly mobs at work in London as in the colonies. Over the last few years, I have seen, at the centre of the mischief-making, some dangerous men on both sides of the Atlantic. If there was an unwillingness to make concessions in the Board of Trade and in the chief servants in its employ in London; if that devil Wilkes sought notoriety and was ready to pay any price for it in London like his one-time crony Wedderburn; so there were dangerous men on this side, too, men like Ebenezer Macintosh and Isaac Sears who would lead out a mob for a handful of small change. I am far from sure that Sam Adams was motivated by anything more than notoriety. His whole career has been nothing but a failure. There are plotters at work in both our countries.

I misjudged quite a few people, among them dreamy-eyed idealists like young Tom Jefferson and wild men pretending to be trained lawyers like Patrick Henry. When I was in Scotland I learnt some apt Scottish terms, and I would use them to describe John Adams who is unco' guid; he will correct God when he—as he assuredly will—goes to meet Him. And I would use that other delightful Scottish phrase—perjink—to describe my Pennsylvanian friends John Dickinson and Joseph Galloway. They are honourable and dedicated men but dry, a bit stuffy, a bit humourless, given—like John Adams—to enjoying and savouring a good conceit of themselves. And there is Arthur Lee: not perjink and not unco' guid, but arrogant, extravagant—and devious. I became worried on my return to the colonies last year about the company I now saw at work. They were young and inexperienced. Had I not had a plan, things might have gone badly for us all. I hate mobs and mob-leaders and I deplore revolutions. Would you were here and we could stage a little revolution all to ourselves and forget the world!

I detect also another awkward and disruptive personality being thrown in to stir the pot even thicker: Tom Paine. I befriended him in London when he had lost his job. He began life as a stay-maker, and became an excise man. He called on me in Craven Street: poor, slovenly, dirty and disreputable, and given to drink, but with a keen mind, ill-educated but well-read in an untidy way, and keen to write. I helped him with his passage over. He has written to say that he is settling down.

But what he does not say is that he nearly died on the journey and when his ship berthed he was lying in a high fever and unconscious. The ship's captain found on him my letter of introduction to my old friend John Kearsley, who had by that time died. Kearsley's nephew of the same name tended him and gave him lodging, but Tom Paine has hounded him mercilessly since, on the grounds of his loyalism, and reports are that the younger Kearsley is now held to be insane.

Paine is a restless and unreliable fellow. He has shown me the draft of his latest pamphlet which he calls 'Common Sense'. It is strong stuff and visits all the blame on the King. This is a great nonsense and will do nothing but inflame opinion. I told him so, but I suspect it will be printed. It will do nothing to cool tempers on either side of the ocean and is but a way of his getting rid of his spleen. I brought him over. I wish I had not. It is but one more of my now many errata. Happily the issue is now resolved.

It was this same misjudgement on my part that led me into passing on the letters of Governor Hutchinson to Speaker Cushing in Boston. Here, too, a little more prescience on my part might have enabled me to remain in a position to prevent relations between England and the Colonies from deteriorating as far as they did. But then, I could hardly have anticipated that the investigation into the letters and their accuracy would turn into a vendetta against me and would present me as the great incendiary of the American cause. You will recall that the letters had been sent by Governor Hutchinson to Thomas Whately in 1768 and that they made clear, it seemed to me, how autocratic he sought to be as an administrator in Massachusetts. They came into the hands of John Temple and they then reached me. When I read them I thought it proper to pass them on to Thomas Cushing, whose agent after all I was, so that he could, in fact, see that one source of our problems lay with Governor Hutchinson and not in London. I had no positive idea of their origin. I assumed they had been stolen, and I know how much the reading of other people's letters was indulged in in London—my own included. But I did not want them to become public property, nor did I expect them to be. Secrets of this sort should be kept. The letters were not in themselves especially dangerous but would give Cushing some ammunition to use. When, however, it became plain that William Whately, the brother and executor of Thomas, had had one duel with John Temple and that there was to be another, I thought it proper—and indeed honourable—to save John Temple's skin by revealing that I and not he had sent them to Boston. The Lord Advocate, Old Sawney, as we called him, had a field day. I was there, as I knew, to be blackened. I was called 'the first mover and prime conductor', 'the actor and secret spring'. I was made to appear the arch organizer of rebellion, which I was not, and the next day I was dismissed from my posts.

I knew, of course, all about Old Sawney,[17] and as a politician with a thick skin I could discount much of his language. Junius called him 'wary', Shelburne was shattered at his 'scurrilous invective', others called him by more savage names like 'ratting'. His switch in 1771 from the cause of Wilkes to that of North was designed to obtain the solicitor-generalship and (I am sure) ultimately the Lord Chancellorship. He sells himself cheap. He had learnt the ruthlessness of his debating techniques in Edinburgh, and in the Kirk; he had moved from Scottish to English seats, cultivated both Wilkes and Clive and even learnt the arts of eloquence and dramatics (and an English accent) from the elder Sheridan. I discounted the histrionics. The crowd turned up just for the show. He is a rough Scottish adventurer on the make and there are a lot of them around, seeking good jobs as placemen, Tories in Tory England, Whigs in lawyer-ridden Edinburgh and—secretly and all the time—Jacobites and Scottish Nationalists. Much can be done with a Scotsman—Poor Richard might have said long before Dr Johnson—if you catch him young. The noblest prospect for a Scot—was it Boswell or Johnson who said it? —is the high road to England. He will do well, Old Sawney, with his Scottish toughness hidden behind a smooth and polished accent.

I lost my job as a result, but I had been down before. And
this time there was an important dividend. Lord Chatham
thought the performance disgusting, and saw how, for once,
the cards had been stacked against me. In August he asked if
he could see me. It proved to be, I believe, a turning point.

You will no doubt be all agog by this time to know how, if I
made these misjudgements, how at the eleventh hour I believe
I have averted the clash which so many expected. It was due, of
course, to two people, Chatham and Lord Howe, or if you like
to the English liking for tea. *Dulce et decorum est desipere in
loco*, as Poor Richard would not have known how to say.
'Lady' Howe invited me to tea and chess. We talked of peace
and I met her brother Lord Howe, already a hero on this side.
I am sure that she invited me in order to meet her brother—I
would have come back otherwise. We agreed on a formula,
and the King, thanks to his family links with the Howe family,
is thought sympathetic to the terms. I never had the honour of
an audience, but I understand that this is in the future.

What then bedevilled things, of course, was the broad
Atlantic. I did not sail until March 1775 and did not reach
Philadelphia until May, with my plan kept carefully secret.
Those six weeks nearly wrecked everything. For during that
time there came those dreadful and ugly incidents at Lexington
and Concord—where, again, small mobs got out of control—
and the still uglier and open battle at Bunker Hill followed a
month later. I had not reckoned on these, nor on Colonel
Washington's going north to Cambridge to form an army.
It almost seemed that events might go too quickly for me,
especially as, within 24 hours, I was elected to the Continental
Congress. That touch of popularity worried me too, although
it gave me contact with some key people. Some were helpful.
Some—I will leave you to guess who—were very stupid.

The Congress knew of my plan, of course, and of the authority
I was charged to wield. The deal turned on Colonel Washington
and this was the real reason why I went north last October,
though it was disguised as a 'Congressional Inspection'. The
plan was to abandon the Proclamation Line of 1763 and its

various amendments, and the Quebec Act with it. It became clear that the Line was not holding, and with Pontiac's rebellion in 1763 and then the War fought by Governor Dunmore with the Shawnee in 1774, there was clearly no hope of real peace with the Indians. Shelburne's hopes of averting this clash were weakened. This—and I would like to think our steady demands for a western colony—led Lord North to agree to the fourteenth colony of Vandalia being set up. And Vandalia it is to be—not, I am happy to say, the various fanciful names young Tom Jefferson suggested.[18]

I had the pleasure of telling the Colonel this, and of offering the governorship to him. I will never forget the reaction. He never hesitated. 'I am no revolutionary,' he said. As for this so-called Army of Yankees: 'They are an exceeding dirty and nasty people.'[19] He plans as soon as his official appointment is confirmed to move to Fort Pitt as his base and Martha is going to join him. The replacement of General Gage by William Howe and his brother the Earl was designed, of course, to bring another peacemaker to Boston. The two army commanders met at Boston Neck, and I was able to point to some of my boyhood haunts and swimming holes to both of them. General Howe sent some of his veterans to help Colonel Washington but was happy to sail back home with most of them. He sailed back on July 4, 1776, a day for that reason we should celebrate in the future.

The British have, as you know, withdrawn the tea tax and the coercive Acts—aided by my offer to pay for the tea—I hope the Congress will find the £16,000 I pledged! The Acts would never have been passed if the Tea Party had not happened, and that is something we must blame, I fear, on Thomas Hutchinson. He could have let the ships go: those at New York and Charleston provoked no crisis. Hutchinson was the holder of a tea concession and was in fact seeking a profit. I am sorry for the man: courageous, dedicated, sincere, a critic of the Stamp Act, who got the mob wrecking his home for his pains, he has not been lucky, but—frankly—he is a snob, out of touch with people. He has wisely decided to stay behind in London, but has refused a baronetcy. His heart aches, I know, for Boston but I doubt if he will ever return.

Washington will accept a baronetcy and will play the part to perfection—even though it is rather pointless, since he has no children.

I made one concession and it will be difficult to push through. I agreed that we undertook to make a contribution to defence, because it is clear that we need defending. It is defence against Indians but there are also other alien groups, not least the Germans in Western Pennsylvania. (I wish for my part that we were more British and less mixed as a people.)[20] The trouble is that if we are to contribute to our own defence, as I think we should, we will probably need to have a Congress permanently sitting on this side of the water. This leaves me uneasy. Separate Parliaments mean power to tax and are likely to lead to separation. The Scots could tell us something here—they abandoned their faction-riddled Parliament in 1707 to secure seats in London, and wise men they were to do so. The nature of the financial contribution will have to be looked at calmly, and I think over there rather than here. It is clear that in the Congress counsels are vastly diverse and conflicting. Connecticut talks of a tax on the import of Negroes, because—as you know—it has few. This is in fact not at all a bad idea, but it will be unwelcome south of the Chesapeake. No doubt Southerners will reply with a tax on molasses, and why not? Why not both?

I count myself especially fortunate in being put on the small Committee that was set up to draft what might otherwise have become something we might have had to call a Declaration of Independence. That demand came from that hot-headed family, the Lees of Virginia. They saw Jefferson as their spokesman. I was glad to let him have the job, though he did not relish it, and was constantly agitating to get back to his beloved Monticello and his wife, who seems to be endlessly pregnant. He rushed the job and produced a strange abstract draft. I joked over it, knowing that this was no more than a piece of paper. I hardly trusted myself to keep cool with him, since he is ultra-sensitive to criticism, but his document, albeit elegantly and sonorously and even rhetorically written needs a rebuttal. In fact, writing under the pseudonym 'Englishman', I sent off to *The Gentleman's Magazine* my own comments on his paper. I hope that paper prints it, as it is Mr Burke's vehicle of opinion in London.[21]

I am glad I persuaded the Congress to adopt, instead of Mr Jefferson's draft, our Declaration of Interdependence.

Why, I hear you say, why have it printed in London? The reason is that I am to return there. I have left this news to the end, believing (and hoping) that it will cause you distress. It will be my seventh crossing. And—I now write only for you—I am to wear ermine. So I shall expect a deep and obedient curtsey when we meet, and for my part regret only that the feudal *droit de seigneur* does not accompany the peerage that Chatham has persuaded the King to grant. My pleasure lies in the real opportunity to voice the American cause there and to speak no longer pleadingly as a colonial agent. If there had been enough of us there three years ago this silly threat of secession would never have arisen. For just as I believe that in science there is no problem that cannot be resolved by diligence, patience and reason, so I hold that in politics those same qualities, and goodwill, will find solutions. Secession from this growing Empire would have been a disaster. Unions, once achieved, should never be destroyed without much careful thought.

I affect in public a modesty about the honour that secretly I find it hard to sustain. I am in fact very proud. It cancels, and is meant to cancel the insults of the Cockpit. It salutes the long years of struggle. My friend Sandwich, who sits in the Lords as Lord Despencer, says that I should take the title Lord of Misrule. Less genial spirits call me Lord Doubleface. It will probably be simply Franklin of Philadelphia. And it will permit me also to end another rumour that I have not, until now, bothered even to contradict. For William will succeed me in the title at the King's special request.[22] He has been an admirable Governor of New Jersey and came equally admirably through the trials of his short imprisonment in

Connecticut. He is of course legitimate, but when he was born, Deborah, his mother, was still in form married to the wastrel who we thought might return and who, if he had returned, could have made things difficult for us both. That is why we married at common law. But the Franklins of Ecton in Northampton, leather-apron men and of the people, have reached the purple. What would Poor Richard say?

Lord Howe will of course stay on to serve as the King's Viceroy. I am officially sailing not to England but to France, under the guise of seeking their support. I do not want that support, for that would indeed be to invite disaster; to leap from the frying pan to the fire. All that the King has to do is to agree to our suggestions. The task of conciliation will of course not be quick. We need 7 to 10 years.[23]

Pray for me, for you, I know, believe in prayer. Pray also for America. As I pray for both.[24]

Your friend,

Benjamin Franklin

3

The letter of course is fanciful. Every reference in it to the facts, however, is accurate, as the footnotes attest. The expedition to Canada did take place and he did dislike it; he did visit Washington's headquarters in October 1775, though not to talk of peace; he did spend hours in 1775 in talks with 'Lady' Howe and her brother, and with Lord Chatham and there were still conversations between Howe and Franklin in 1776. Had Chatham not become by then the supreme egotist, had the Howes been a little closer to the King—and they were close, being (illegitimate) blood relatives—had he himself been a little more trusted by the men around North. . . .

It can of course always be argued that even had this most smooth of all negotiators averted separation in 1776, there could be no guarantee that in every generation and in every subsequent crisis between the two countries, a man of Franklin's skill and facility would always have appeared 'at the eleventh hour' as he puts it, to pour oil on troubled water—which was incidently one of his favourite party tricks.[25] Maybe not. But is it necessary to hold that there was any real inevitability in Anglo-American separation? Franklin's vision of a transatlantic Empire of trade and growth was a noble one. The ties of trade by 1790 were almost as close, despite formal political separation, as they had been in 1770. The ties of culture remain as close as those that obtain inside many national boundaries. War was no prerequisite for cultural identity. Canada grew to independence without any need for a War of Independence. From whatever Kingdom of Hell or Heaven to which this sceptical, genial and lovable Deist went, he is likely to have watched all subsequent history with nostalgia, and still to be saying—or is it Poor Richard who speaks?—'What fools those mortals were.'

NOTES

1 Benjamin Franklin first met Catherine Ray (1731–94) in Boston in 1754. He was 48, she was 23. He was in the North as Deputy Postmaster General, she was visiting her sister Judith, the wife of Thomas Hubbard, stepson of Franklin's brother John, whom he appointed Postmaster of Boston in December 1754.

They appear to have travelled south together, on a journey of 70 miles to Newport, involving one night in an inn *en route*, and then to have travelled to Catherine's sister Anne at Westerly, before parting at Point Judith. They would seem to have been therefore 17 or 18 days in each other's company. Block Island was 12 miles off shore. All 3 of her sisters were married, and Catherine returned to nurse her sick father aged 82, who died in March 1755.

Both would often recall the journey together, how they talked away the hours 'on a winter journey on a wrong road and in a soaking shower', the horses 'no more able to stand than if they had been shod on skates'.

She wrote him three letters—March 31, March 31 and April 28, 1755 (the last accompanied by a gift of sugar plums)—which all the assiduity of the editors of the Franklin Papers at Yale has failed to unearth. Presumably, Franklin destroyed them, although this was for him a very rare step; it is legitimate to guess that they said more than he cared to have preserved. His own letters in reply, though warm, have what is for him a guarded quality. He was seeking to play an avuncular role, though it did not perhaps come naturally. 'Love me,' she wrote, 'one thousandth Part so well as I do you.' 'Though you say more,' he replied, 'I say less than I think.' This was to be the first, though not the last, of his *amitiés amoureuses*. His letter to her, March 4, 1755, written before receipt of hers and immediately on his return to Philadelphia, suggests the closeness of the affection. 'I thought so much was hazarded when I saw you put off to sea in that very little skiff, tossed by every wave. I stood on the shore and looked after you till I could no longer distinguish you even with my glass. . . . You have spun a long thread, 5022 yards! . . . I wish I had hold of one end of it to pull you to me.'

2 Catherine Ray married William Greene (1731–1809), a second cousin.

3 Franklin's wife, Deborah Read, died December 1774, 6 months before Franklin's return to America.

4 Her cousin Betty Greene seems to have found Franklin's language too outspoken when he visited the family in October 1775, during his visit to Washington's headquarters at Cambridge. Catherine Greene seems later to have quarrelled with Betty—perhaps over her friendship for Benjamin Franklin, or over Betty's charge that Franklin had made approaches to her also?

5 Franklin was miserable on his northern expedition, and his letters are remarkably taciturn about it. Congress appointed a commission of three men to solicit support in Canada and even encourage a rebellion there in sympathy with that in the Colonies. They left New York by boat, April 2, and reached Montreal through snow and ice on April 29. The mission was hopeless: the French Canadians were hostile, the American army short of cash and food, British reinforcements were arriving at Quebec. He returned to New York, which he reached on May 27, low in spirit and complaining of gout.

6 Franklin misquoted himself. In his letter to Lord Howe, January 30, 1776, *Writings of Benjamin Franklin*, Vol 6. (1907), he spoke of that 'fine and noble vase, the British Empire'.

7 *Observations concerning the Increase of Mankind* was published 1751, *Papers*, Vol. IV, pp. 225–234 (1961).

8 William Franklin (1731–1813), illegitimate son of Benjamin Franklin, was Governor of New Jersey 1762–1776 and became a Loyalist.

9 To Lord Kames, January 30, 1760, *Papers*, Vol. 9, p. 9 (1966).

10 William Beckford (1709–70), Member of Parliament for the City of London 1754 to 1770, was a wealthy Jamaica sugar merchant and a supporter of Wilkes. He served as Lord Mayor in 1762 and again in 1769.

11 See Franklin's pamphlet, *The Interests of Great Britain considered with Regard to her Colonies and the Acquisition of Canada and Guadeloupe, Writings*, ed. Smyth, Vol. IV, pp. 32–82 (1907); *Papers*, Vol. IX, pp. 47–100 (1966).

12 An all-too-inaccurate forecast. Only for a few months in 1784 was there hope of his name being thus preserved. But 'the lost state of Franklin' in Tennessee did not last.

13 John Pownall (1720–95), Secretary of the Board of Trade, 1758–76, and also Undersecretary of State for the Colonies, 1768–76; Commissioner of Excise, 1776.

14 William Petty, first Marquess of Lansdowne and second Earl of Shelburne (1737–1805), served as President of the Board of Trade under Grenville, 1763, and as Secretary of State for the Southern Department under Pitt in 1766–68. He was a critic of American policies thereafter, until in 1783 as first Lord of the Treasury he signed the Treaty of Peace which recognized American independence. Although Franklin found him congenial, he was held to be untrustworthy, primarily because he shared Pitt's scorn for party groups.

   The fifteenth Baron Le Despencer (1708–81) is better known as the Sir Francis Dashwood who founded the Hell-fire Club or the Society of the Monks of Medmenham Abbey in c. 1755. He served as Chancellor of the Exchequer, 1763–1760, and as Joint Postmaster General from 1770 until his death.

15 Cadwallader Colden (1688–1776) was born in Ireland of Scots ancestry. Scientist and doctor of medicine, he was also land surveyor and public official, and from 1761 until 1776 served as Lieutenant-Governor (and occasionally as acting Governor) of New York.

16 Governor Thomas Hutchinson (1711–80), Lieutenant-Governor, 1758, and Chief Justice of Massachusetts Bay, 1760; Governor, 1771–74; his removal was petitioned for by Massachusetts Assembly after disclosure (1773) by Franklin of private letters to Whately written in 1768–9. Although these letters expressed no views that had not been already made plain, it was now clear that he was secretly urging the home government to exert its authority more vigorously. In 1773 he unwisely used his influence to obtain tea consignments for his sons, Thomas and Elisha, whose tea business he largely directed. By refusing to give the tea ships clearance papers until the tea was landed, he played into Sam Adams's hands. In 1774 he left for England to report to the King. As the years dragged on, he was desperately homesick but never returned. He died in June 1780 and is buried in Croydon.

17 The hearing before the Privy Council in the Cockpit on January 29, 1774, was on the petition of the Massachusetts House to remove Governor Hutchinson. Because of the letters, however—and unhappily coinciding with the first reports of the Boston Tea Party— Solicitor General Alexander Wedderburn ('Old Sawney') transformed this occasion into an attack on Franklin as a thief, a man without honour, and the ringleader in the rebellion brewing in Boston. Next day Franklin was deprived of his postmastership. He recognized that he was now seen as a dangerous man and as an enemy. For him, aged 68, it seemed the end of a career.

18 Congress approved Jefferson's plan for the settlement of the North West but not the names proposed for ten of the potential states: Cherronesus, Polypotamia, Pelipsia, Assenenisipia, Metropotamia now seem eccentric and provoked much ridicule. To an age more familiar both with Indian and classical names perhaps they seemed less strange.

19 Washington's comments on the Yankees were indeed outspoken. 'Their officers,' he wrote to his cousin and estate manager, Lund Washington, 'are generally speaking the most indifferent kind of people I ever saw ... I dare say the men would fight very well if properly officered although they are an exceeding dirty and nasty people' (Washington, *Writings*, Vol. III, pp. 309, 433, Vol. IV, pp. 320: ed. J. C. Fitzpatrick, Washington DC, 1931–44).

20 Benjamin Franklin was a critic of non-British immigration, especially of the 'Palatine boors' and the Germans in the west of his state. His criticisms were used against him in the bitterly-fought election in Pennsylvania in 1764 when he lost his seat in the Assembly.

21 It was indeed printed:
'We hold, they say, these truths to be self-evident: That all men are created equal. In what are they created equal? Is it in size, strength, understanding, figure, moral or civil accomplishments, or situation of life? Every plough-man knows that they are not created equal in any of these. All men, it is true, are equally created, but what is this to the purpose? It certainly is no reason why the Americans should turn rebels because the people of Great Britain are their fellow-creatures, i.e. are created as well as themselves. It may be a reason why they should not rebel, but most indisputably is none why they should. They therefore have introduced their self-evident truths, either through ignorance, or by design, with a self-evident falsehood: since I will defy any American rebel, or any of their patriotic retainers here in England,

to point out to me any two men, throughout the whole World, of whom it may with truth be said that they are created equal. . . .

An Englishman'
in *The Gentleman's Magazine,* Vol. XLVI (September 1776), p. 403.

22 Relations between father and son were in fact permanently broken by the outbreak of the War. No one knows who William's mother was. It might well have been Deborah.

23 The possibilities of conciliation certainly existed. In November 1774, Franklin wrote, half ironically, an *Intended Speech* for the King to deliver, and in it he suggested that the task of conciliation would require seven to ten years. He listed a number of proposals: the tea to be paid for (and he did offer to pay for it himself if the coercive acts were repealed); the Navigation Acts to be re-enacted in the colonial legislatures, and the duties arising from them to be available 'for public use'; America to maintain its own military establishment and there would be voluntary grants from the colonies in time of war; and the Quebec Act to be repealed.

24 Benjamin Franklin and Catherine Ray Greene continued to correspond —his last letter to her was written March 2, 1789—but they never met after 1776. He died in 1790 and she in 1794.

25 While a guest of Lord Shelburne's at his estate in High Wycombe, April 1772—in company with David Garrick, Colonel Barré and the Abbé Morellet—Franklin quietened the water of the lake by waving his cane over it. In the hollow of his cane he had usefully stored a quantity of oil. Morellet, *Memoires inédits,* Vol. I, pp. 197–204; Franklin, *Papers,* Vol. 19, p. 177.

If I had been . . .

BENITO JUÁREZ IN 1867

'How I would have pardoned the Emperor Maximilian—and, perhaps, have saved Mexico from decades of political and social turmoil.'

PETER CALVERT

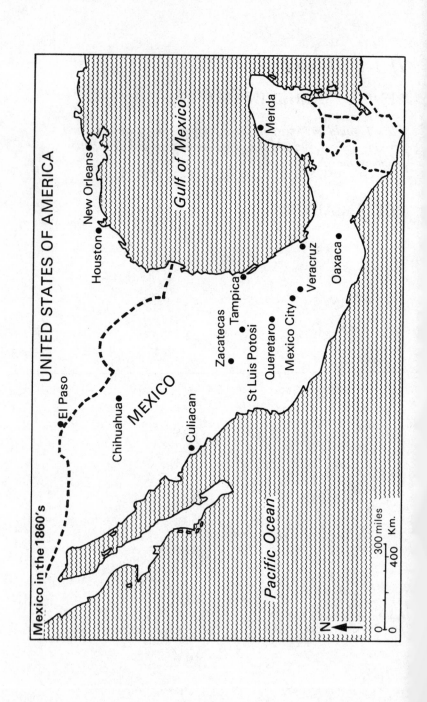

1

In the spring of 1867 the city of Querétaro in North Central Mexico became briefly the last capital of Mexico's second Empire. The Empire had formally come into existence only three years before, in 1864, when the Archduke Maximilian of Austria had accepted the offer of the crown of Mexico from a delegation of Mexican Conservatives. The Conservatives, led by the youthful soldier Miguel Miramón, had been defeated by the Liberals, under the lawyer and civilian President Benito Juárez, in a Three Years War between 1858 and 1861. But the divided state of Mexico, and the fact that the United States to the north was by then engaged in its own Civil War, had tempted the Emperor Napoleon III of France to send his forces there, nominally to collect unpaid debts of very dubious legality, but in practice to carve out a French protectorate in the New World. Within months the French forces had apparently been successful, and the rump Republican government under Benito Juárez had been forced to retreat to the far northern frontier of the country where they continued to maintain their resistance. Disregarding them, the French and their Conservative allies then proceeded to make their conquest secure by proclaiming the Empire, and selected Maximilian of Austria as they had no eligible candidate of their own.

When the tall, blond Maximilian and his Empress, Carlota— both attractive and only in their early thirties—reached Mexico, they were charmed by it. The French forces were able to maintain order throughout most of Mexico, and they soon captured the most dangerous Republican general in the south, Porfirio Díaz, and locked him up. Many prominent Mexicans surrounded the throne, especially the 'Four M's'—Generals Miramón, Márquez, Méndez, and Mejía—and they brought with them small numbers of enthusiastic followers. But it was not long before things began to go wrong. For one thing, it became sadly plain to Maximilian that the elections on which he had insisted before accepting the crown had been rigged. Worse still, Maximilian, who for an Austrian was a Liberal, found his Conservative allies unbelievably reactionary, and they in turn found him weak.

The American Civil War came to an end in 1865 and the United States was free at last to object to French colonization in the New World. Not long afterwards, Porfirio Díaz made a daring escape from captivity, and resumed the war in the south of Mexico, while soon, with better supplies from the United States and new recruits, the tide of war began to turn in the north also. Ultimately, under heavy pressure from the United States and fearful at home for the rising power of Prussia in Europe, Napoleon III agreed to withdraw his forces from Mexico, though already it was clear that the Mexican Imperialists were too few and too divided to replace them. The Empress Carlota herself went to Europe to plead with Napoleon; under the strain her mind began to give way. One of the last acts of the French commander, Marshal Bazaine, before sailing from Mexico was to send word on February 13, 1867 to Maximilian at Mexico City that the way was still open for him and his staff to join him on board ship. The message was not delivered. Maximilian had already taken the decision to abandon the capital and join the last major Imperial Army, that of General Miramón, at Querétaro, where he hoped to rally more support and counterattack.

At the beginning of March the Republican forces under General Escobedo established a siege there. They were unable to make it fully effective, at first for lack of manpower, and the Imperial General Márquez, whom Maximilian had created Lieutenant General of the Empire, managed to break out towards Mexico City in search of reinforcements. Having obtained them, however, he failed to return, and instead was invested in the capital by the forces of Porfirio Díaz. Informing Maximilian of this turn of events, the Republican general offered him his freedom if he surrendered his armies, but Maximilian refused. Two weeks later, on the night of May 14–15, the city of Querétaro was betrayed to the Republicans by a Colonel López. In the fighting, General Miramón was wounded and surrendered to the Republicans. The Emperor and General Mejía were captured at the head of their forces on the Hill of Bells to the west of the city.

Juárez, waiting impatiently at San Luis Potosí, 140 miles further north, received the news the same day. Later, when asked what was to be done with the prisoners, he directed that they be tried where they were by court martial. After a delay, granted by Juárez to permit the defendants to obtain lawyers from the beleagured capital, the trial was held from July 11–13, and all three defendants, found guilty of being in arms against the Republic, were sentenced to death by a 4 to 3 majority. Following frantic appeals from many sources, Juárez conceded them a three-day reprieve to put their affairs in order, but refused to pardon them, and on the morning of July 19, Maximilian and the two Mexican generals were led out to execution on the Hill of Bells. Maximilian, who the previous day had sent a last message asking that he alone suffer, supported Mejía, who was weak through illness, and ceded the place of honour in the centre to Miramón. He fell at the first volley.

The executions at Querétaro ended Mexican Conservatism as such. As a result, Juárez was undisputed leader of Mexico until his death in 1872; he paved the way for Porfirio Díaz, who ruled Mexico almost without interruption from 1877 to 1911, when the social forces so long held in check by his dictatorship erupted in the Mexican Revolution, one of the first of the great revolutions that have shaped our own century, in which at least half a million Mexicans died. But suppose Maximilian had lived. . . .

Let us go back to the day of the fall of Querétaro and see the situation unfold from the viewpoint of Juárez. Could he have decided to let Maximilian live? Let us imagine that he has just heard of the arrest of Maximilian. It is 4.15 in the afternoon and he has just finished a letter to his family, so he adds the news in a bare sentence with a 'Viva México!', seals the paper and sends it out to the post orderly. Then, alone in that bare room, he becomes aware of the unease behind the joy that the news has given him.

2

But what a heroic fool that Austrian princeling is! Did he not realize that he will have to die? Mind you, he would have had no hesitation in ordering *my* execution if our positions were reversed. And how nearly they were, only five months ago at Zacatecas, when I escaped in the nick of time! When our men retook Zacatecas they found an order, with the Austrian's signature on it, directing that traitor Miramón to try me and my ministers if he were to capture us, and to refer the sentence to Maximilian himself. And what else could he have done then but to have us shot, with the traitors baying for blood?

Martial law is no law? Perhaps, but it is all we Mexicans have left. Sudden executions have been all too familiar in this poor country of late. Back in 1862, I issued a decree to the effect that all who aided the French intervention, Mexicans or foreigners, were to be considered traitors, liable to the death penalty by court martial. But Maximilian issued an even more severe decree in 1865 ordering the summary execution of all persons caught bearing arms against his so-called Empire—even women and children. Under it, two of our finest generals were executed only days later. Many others have followed since. And of course our uneducated soldiers, on both sides, have frequently shot people of all ranks out of hand. Personally I take a dim view of this. As a lawyer dedicated to the maintenance of the Law, I draw a sharp distinction between leaders and followers. What was it that I wrote to Porfirio last March?

'It seems to me well for you to follow your accustomed rule of not shooting the enlisted men who fall prisoner, whether they are Mexicans or foreigners, except when you find among them some whose known acts make them worthy of the penalty of death, in which case they should not go unpunished. As for the prominent leaders, commanders and officers involved in aggravating circumstances, they should be dealt with with the full rigor of the law.'

Of course Escobedo may have Maximilian shot out of hand, but I doubt it. He is too big a fish. Besides, these soldiers stick together; if they can let one another escape they always do. And there is the problem for the government. This is a political question. We hold the Court cards—how can we play them so as to bring peace to Mexico most quickly? Patience, and shuffle the cards.

How ironical that I, Benito Juárez, who come of the pure Indian stock of the state of Oaxaca, where we resisted the Spaniards to the last, should now have as my captive Maximilian of Habsburg—the distant descendant of the Emperor Charles V, King of Spain when Cortés came! Is four centuries of suffering at last to be brought to an end? I fervently hope so . . .

. . . I gather that when Maximilian was arrested, he informed General Escobedo, before whom he was brought, that he had already signed his abdication. (What happened to it, I do not know; he said he had given it to Márquez, but that old fox had not seen fit at that time to make it public.) He then undertook, if he were given an escort, to leave the country immediately, with all his European followers, never to return. Quite properly, General Escobedo told him that this request would have to be referred to higher authority, whereupon the Austrian surrendered unconditionally. The request has now come before me, together with the disposition of Miramón and Mejía.

With Márquez still holding the capital, to release Maximilian, even under heavy guard, would plainly endanger the whole structure of peace, so laboriously sought and hoped for. Bazaine and the French sailed from Mexico in mid-March, so Maximilian would remain the central focus for Conservative

intrigues while he awaits the next ship. And he *has* been keeping
bad company! Against Mejía I have nothing special except his
defence of an obsolete cause. He has resisted the advancing tide
of human progress which has already carried our century far
beyond the achievements of any of its predecessors.

But Miramón is a different question. He has betrayed both
his country and the Republic (though he has sworn, in his own
fashion, to uphold both them and the Law itself). In doing so,
he has ceased to be, as he had been when he led the Conservatives in the Three Years War, a gallant partisan leader and
a brave if not altogether scrupulous enemy. He has become
instead only the latest of the traitors who throughout our
history have betrayed our country to foreigners. And that puts
him in the line of such notables as La Malinche, the Indian
woman who was mistress and interpreter to Cortés; the priests
who sentenced Father Hidalgo, the first to give voice to
Mexico's cry for independence and to call on us Indians to rid
ourselves of the Spanish yoke; Agustín de Iturbide, who freed
Mexico from the Spaniards only to try to make himself Emperor,
and who, when allowed to leave the country with wealth and
honour intact by our infant Republic, conspired with his former
enemies and tried to return (and was executed for his treachery!);
and Antonío López de Santa Anna, eleven times President in
our turbulent first half-century of independence, who in 1849
had lost over half our national territory to the United States,
and yet in 1853 when they asked for more, sold it to them, and
pocketed the money.

You can't blame the foreigners for the recurrent tragedies
our country has faced, as much as those Mexicans who have
betrayed it at every turn. The only way to end this sorry state
of affairs is to deal out exemplary justice, so that none should
be tempted to betray Mexico again in future. Ideally this should
be done in the capital, but that as yet eludes the grasp of our
Republican troops. There is no point in bringing the prisoners
120 miles north over appalling roads to San Luis Potosí for
trial. Our Law of January 5, 1862 provides for all three
prisoners, Mexican or foreign, to be tried by court martial

where they are. So I have directed General Escobedo, by letter, to make arrangements for the trial as soon as possible . . .

. . . On receiving news of the order, Maximilian wrote personally to me to ask for an interview. He has done so before, at the beginning of the French intervention in our affairs, when it was the Republican cause that seemed lost. It irritates me to be drawn into these tricky situations. On how many occasions have I not been tempted to abandon hope and settle for a quiet life in exile! Anxious to maintain what impartiality I can in what is, after all, an essentially judicial process, I have merely directed that the prisoners should prepare their defence.

My next reminder of the prisoners of Querétaro comes from an unexpected source, the young American-born wife of a Prussian soldier-of-fortune who had loyally remained with his Emperor. Princess zu Salm-Salm, her dress dusty and torn from her difficult journey, has turned up to plead with me for Maximilian to be given a fortnight more before his trial. She had already been to plead on behalf of her husband, against whom we had no special charges, and I find I am moved as much by her courage as by her arguments. I listen to her courteously and, making up my mind at once, telegraph to General Escobedo to suspend all proceedings for a fortnight. This will give time for lawyers to be fetched from the capital, occupied as it still is by Maximilian's own men. It does, I must admit, cross my mind too that it might also give Maximilian's supporters time to plan his escape, but this doesn't worry me overmuch as, by now, our armies are triumphing on all fronts.

As it later transpires, there is a plot for an escape, planned for the evening of June 2. But when the appointed day arrives, it seems that the Emperor, though all the arrangements have been made, refuses to make the attempt because the lawyers and the diplomatic corps are due to come to see him the next day. The guards, of course, are unable to conceal their new wealth in the *cantina*, and General Escobedo, when he gets to hear of the escape plot, can hardly do less than to remove all other

prisoners from the building and expel all foreigners from the
town . . .

. . . The postponed date for the trial eventually arrives. The
proceedings take place in a theatre before 1500 people between
June 11 and 13. Maximilian is not present, officially because of
illness, but his defence is presented by four of the leading
lawyers of the country. I must own that as a lawyer I am anxious
about this, since it is a good defence, and from what I hear it is
not effectively refuted by the prosecutor. However the sound
points of law on which it is based are scarcely within the understanding of the board of young and inexperienced officers which
General Escobedo has clearly appointed in order to ensure a
conviction. They agree at once that the defendants are guilty,
but are so overawed by their responsibility that it is only after
a long discussion, and after the President has had to use his
casting vote, that they decide on the death penalty rather than
banishment. On the morning of June 16, General Escobedo's
message conveying the decision reaches me. It states that the
sentence will be carried out at three o'clock the same afternoon.

Two of the lawyers defending Maximilian are already at
San Luis Potosí, where they come to see me. I take the news
calmly. With the capital still in enemy hands, there is a need for
an exemplary demonstration of the Law. Who knows? News
of the execution might be the one thing needed to cause the
surrender of Márquez and save needless suffering.

'The government acts by necessity on this occasion, denying
the humanitarian sentiments of which it has given and will still
give innumerable proofs,' I tell them. 'The law and the sentence
are inexorable now, because public safety so demands. It can
also counsel the economy of blood, and that will be the greatest
satisfaction of my life. The tomb of Maximilian and the others
will be the redemption of the rest of the misled.'

They shrug their shoulders and go out without a word, and
I feel exasperated that the foolish young Maximilian had not
made good his escape. I have no personal enmity towards him.

He was largely the dupe of others. On humanitarian grounds I should pardon him there and then. The problem is that humanitarian arguments are not the only ones I have to weigh. Porfirio Díaz has telegraphed that if clemency is granted he would be unable to answer for the sympathies of the army besieging the capital, and in Querétaro itself many of Escobedo's followers threaten to carry out the sentence themselves! It is not I who take his life; it is the people and the Law. If I should not do the will of the Law, the people will take his life, and mine also . . .

. . . I receive a telegram from Baron Magnus, the new Minister of Prussia, the Power whose new strength in Europe has brought about the French withdrawal. Can he come and see me urgently? He can; in fact he has already arrived and is waiting in my anteroom. Time is short, he says, after the briefest of courtesies, and the condemned men have barely time to put their affairs in order. Could I grant a stay of execution? He probably hopes against hope that somehow he can save Maximilian's life. But his request is a legitimate one and I grant it without much thought. My first impulse is to grant only a three-day post-ponement, but as the words form in my mind it occurs to me that that might be too short, so I decide to make it a week.

I have no immediate idea what the outcome of this decision might be. I guess that I will regret it. It occurs to me that it will mean more pleas for mercy, more pain. And I am soon proved right. Within two days I have to receive a delegation of two hundred women from Querétaro, who have, despite the appal-ling conditions, travelled from there to plead for the prisoners' lives, and—most agonizing of all—the wife of Miramón, who brings her two small children and is carried out fainting. Once you allow an exception to be made in the application of the Law, you bring down no end of troubles on your head.

Baron Magnus has been in touch with Europe, and tele-graphs to me that the Emperor of Austria is prepared, with the co-sponsorship of other European rulers, to guarantee that

if Maximilian is freed he will leave the country never to return
and will have no more to do with Mexican affairs. As proof of
this, Emperor Franz Josef has restored Maximilian to his
place second in the succession to the real throne of Austria,
which he had made him renounce on his accepting the shadow
throne of Mexico. It is difficult to resist a feeling of satisfaction
at this new politeness of the Sovereigns of Europe, which we
poor Mexicans have not seen much of lately. I can even ignore
the impertinent suggestion of the United States that an execution
'would not raise the character of Mexico in the esteem of
civilized peoples'. Coming from a country which has just been
devastated by the greatest civil war in history, that is a bit much.
But it reminds me that they have pardoned their leading rebels,
even Jefferson Davis himself. And I am much touched by the
warmth and sympathy behind the pleas for mercy sent by
Garibaldi and Victor Hugo, both my most fervent foreign
supporters against the Empire. 'Never has a more magnificent
opportunity presented itself,' writes Hugo. 'Act, Juárez, so that
civilization may take an immense stride. Abolish the death
penalty from the face of the earth.'

Here indeed is a man who understands what we Liberals
have been fighting for: the cause of civilization itself. Imagine,
then, my joy when I receive the news three days later that at
last our victory is complete. The capital is ours—it has surrendered unconditionally to Porfirio Díaz. There is one small
problem. Somehow the elusive Márquez has taken advantage of
the confusion to escape through our lines. The thought crosses
my mind that perhaps Porfirio knows more about this than he
says in his telegram, but I put it aside. It is time, however you
look at it, to show the world that the government, which has
shown it can be just in war, can also be magnanimous in
victory. No longer can Maximilian, or those who support him,
be a serious threat to the Republic. The country is ours. So I
order a messenger to Querétaro with a pardon for all three
prisoners, effective on their safe conduct to Veracruz and exile.

I am a little apprehensive about how Porfirio will take it.
But from his humane treatment of those defenders of the capital

who have fallen into his hands, it would seem that he shares—
or rather, perhaps, has anticipated?—the general feeling of
magnanimity. Is he just building up support for the future?
I don't know. I tell you, these soldiers, they always stick
together. Anyway, the people like my decision; that I do know.
My reception at every town on the long journey south to
Mexico City is tumultuous, and every step seems to confirm my
instinct for humanity. I put it in a nutshell when I speak from
the balcony of the National Palace after Porfirio's splendid
reception, and tell the assembled troops: 'Among nations, as
among individuals, respect for the right of individuals is peace.'

Looking back now, from retirement in 1872, it is interesting
to see how it all turned out and to think how different things
might have been. That fox Miramón died of his wound, on his
way to the United States, but, as we Mexicans say, he was a
spent cartridge. Mejía was a loyal fool; he followed Maximilian
into exile. As for Maximilian's wife Carlota, she went crazy
at the news of the sentence. She was in Rome at the time to
plead with the Pope, and so became the only woman ever to
spend the night in the Vatican—or so they say. But she was all
right soon enough when her husband got back. A woman's
place is with her husband. Did you hear that Maximilian left a
son in Mexico, by the wife of a gardener in Cuernavaca? I
wonder how he'll turn out.

Porfirio is President now. After my wife died, with the
Republic safe at home and respected abroad, I felt it was time
to go. The young men are so impatient nowadays. I don't
think the Army can be kept out of politics, not yet, but with
Porfirio they have a man they can respect, though I would have
preferred a civilian like me. The Army never liked the way I
disbanded them so quickly at the end of the war. That was a
mistake. But the treasury was empty and the people starving.
It is the people who pay for all . . .

3

And how would things have gone then? What further consequences could have followed if that reprieve had been, not for
three days as it actually was, but for seven?

Juárez has received both praise and execration from historians
for his inflexibility. And poor misguided Maximilian has
achieved in death a degree of nobility, an aura of youthful
martyrdom, which the sentimental and romantic in each generation since then have responded to. Today the tourists who visit
Mexico see the rooms he lived in in Chapultepec Castle, the
tiny courtyard of his retreat at Cuernavaca, or the chapel to
his memory on the Hill of Bells. They learn anew the tragedy of
Maximilian and how poor Carlota went mad, outliving by
more than fifty years all the other actors in the tragedy. Of
Juárez they learn little or nothing. Yet Juárez was one of the
greatest statesmen of the Americas, a man who almost single-
handed, guided and welded together a country on the very
point of dissolution, a country which he came almost to per-
sonify, and which, through him, came not only to accept but to
admire its Indian heritage in a century of European domination.

Why does Juárez get such meagre attention? Is it just because,
as some of Europe's more rabid anti-monarchists seemed to
suggest, he was a splendid barbarian? Hardly. Juárez, though
born of a very poor Indian family in a tiny village in Oaxaca
in 1806, was educated by a Jesuit priest and went on to study
law, imbibing as he did so the new scientific ideas of the nineteenth century. Rejecting the religious domination of Mexican
society along with religion itself, he threw himself as a young
man into Liberal politics. He served as Governor of his state,
as a Cabinet Minister, and as Chief Justice, from which position
he was raised to the Presidency in 1858 by the despairing
resignation of his predecessor. Whatever else he was, the author
of the law which secularized the vast church landholdings of
Mexico and the leader who survived both a three-year civil
war and four years against the forces of the greatest power in
Europe was no barbarian.

A silent man who did not court popularity, he was sustained by the warmth and devotion of his family. Early in the war his wife made her way overland on foot and muleback from Oaxaca to Veracruz to join him. But then she had to take refuge in New Orleans while the government of the Republic was hunted in the northern deserts. In exile their son Pepe died, his health undermined by the poverty in which the family lived, and an older son was killed in the campaigns in the south. In his later years, respected but not admired for the toughness this had imposed on him, Juárez was to make at least two serious political blunders, both of which helped to pave the way for Porfirio Díaz's dictatorship and hence for the eventual Mexican Revolution. One was, in the aftermath of Querétaro, to attempt to amend the Constitution unconstitutionally; the later one was to continue in office in 1872 (admittedly after being re-elected) till he died later the same year. Both set bad precedents for a Díaz who became bitter at being, as he saw it, excluded from the power that was rightfully his. Once he seized it for himself, he was not prepared to relinquish it. It is not too far-fetched, I think, to imagine that if Juárez had been able to pardon Maximilian (and as I have suggested here, Maximilian's execution followed from a series of events largely fortuitous and not deliberate), he might have gained what he never quite achieved—the affection as well as the respect of his people. In which case the nature of Díaz's rule might well have been more flexible and not have led to revolution.

There are times when the mind reels as one tries to imagine oneself in the position of Juárez. The events at Querétaro occurred over a quarter of a century before Costa Rica became the first country in the Americas to abolish capital punishment. Yet in many ways our modern standards of civilization are flouted by acts of barbarism more gross than anything known in those days. The refinements of calculated torture which today disfigure so much of the South American continent were unknown in the Mexico of 1867. General Escobedo, in accordance with the unwritten military code, did offer Maximilian more than one chance of escape, when he could, quite legally, have had him shot out of hand. Once captured, Maximilian could have been tried there and then, but instead every opportunity was given for delay, and his case referred to higher authority. I believe that if Juárez had pardoned Maximilian and the other captives, the Army would not have disputed the decision, whatever the hotheads might have said over their *tequila*.

It is much harder to be sure about what would have happened later on. It seems possible that a stable Republic might have evolved, under which Mexico could have regained strength by her own industry and her people prospered. Had Díaz come to power soon enough, others of his generation could have arisen to share power with him, and to defuse social tension by periodic changes of policy. But the parallels with other Latin American states in this period, though they offer hope that this might have happened, are not altogether encouraging. A more likely scenario seems to be a series of civilian governments punctuated by military coups and short periods of dictatorship. Such a development could have had dangerous consequences. One of those dictators might, for instance, have tried to seek revenge on the United States for the consequences of the Mexican War, and the Mexicans might have succeeded in wresting back Texas and California. Such an outcome is not inconceivable. After all, the United States Army in the early twentieth century had for over a generation been used only to Indian campaigns and minor punitive expeditions, and was dangerously enfeebled and practically incapable of mobilization. It awoke to a sense of its own failings only as a result of the Mexican Revolution of 1911. If that had not taken place, or even been delayed, the United States would probably not have intervened in the Great War. So perhaps it is just as well, after all, that Benito Juárez executed Maximilian in 1867.

If I had been ...

ADOLPHE THIERS IN 1870

'How I would have prevented the Franco-Prussian War.'

MAURICE PEARTON

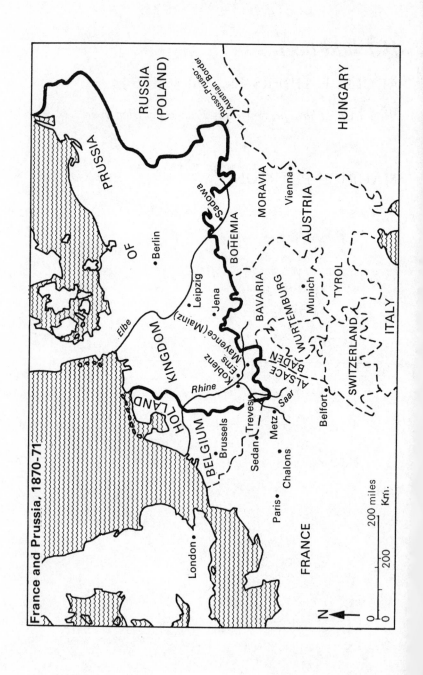

France and Prussia, 1870-71

RUSSIA (POLAND)

PRUSSIA

Russo-Prusso-Austrian Border

Sadowa

Berlin

BOHEMIA

MORAVIA

Vienna

AUSTRIA

HUNGARY

KINGDOM

OF

Elbe

Leipzig

Jena

Mayence (Mainz)

Koblenz

Ems

Rhine

BAVARIA

WURTEMBURG

Munich

BADEN

TYROL

SWITZERLAND

ITALY

HOLLAND

BELGIUM

Brussels

Treves

Sedan

Metz

Saar

ALSACE

Belfort

London

Paris

Chalons

FRANCE

N

200 miles

Km.

0   200

0

1

*At the beginning of 1870, the Empire of Napoleon III seemed to
have accomplished the transition from dictatorship to liberal
constitutionalism and, in its foreign policy, to have come to terms
with Prussia's gains in north Germany and the Rhineland. In mid-
year French policy still seemed set fair for peaceful development.*

On July 2, the Gazette de France *published the news that
Leopold of Hohenzollern, a (distant) relative of the King of
Prussia, had accepted the crown of Spain. The announcement
touched off a stormy and bellicose outcry at the injury to French
honour and interests. The reaction was especially virulent at
Court and in the capital. Napoleon's Foreign Minister, the Duc de
Gramont, furiously threatened war against Prussia if the candidature were not withdrawn: Napoleon quietly negotiated
through the family network; the candidature, manoeuvred
secretly by Bismarck, was withdrawn publicly on July 12. Peace
seemed assured and the international prestige of France was
higher than it had been for a decade. But the war fever was
unassuaged. French generals considered that they had been
deprived of an opportunity to administer long-overdue chastisement to a parvenu power. The streets of Paris concurred. Gramont
instructed his Ambassador to obtain from the King of Prussia a
personal guarantee that he would never permit a renewal of a
Hohenzollern candidature. That demand was refused. The
interview took place at Ems and was reported by telegram to
Bismarck who promptly edited it, to make the refusal appear a*

calculated insult, and gave it to the Press. Bismarck's reading of the psychology of the French leaders was correct. Voices counselling moderation were drowned in the clamour for war to avenge the humiliation France had suffered. On July 15, the Corps Legislatif voted the war credits; four days later, France formally declared war on Prussia.

The expected military promenade to Berlin got no further than Alsace and Lorraine. A continuous offensive by German forces turned French setbacks into defeats and defeats into disasters. The main French field army, with Napoleon himself, surrendered at Sedan on September 2: the other regular force capitulated at Metz on October 29. France paid severely for its impetuous plunge into war, and the process by which Franco-German rivalry brought about the destruction of the European order began.

Among the few who opposed war in July 1870 was Adolphe Thiers (1797–1877), former lawyer, journalist, Prime Minister, political exile and, since 1863, leader of the opposition to Napoleon's dictatorship. He saw, correctly, that Leopold's withdrawal gave France all she wanted: accordingly, there was no need for war: if any ensued it would be brought on by the French government 'over a mere matter of form'. The speech in which he made these points, on July 15, was drowned in catcalls and abuse. At the end of the month, Napoleon, on leaving Paris for the front, offered Thiers the Ministry of War. Thiers refused, and with his refusal disappeared the last possible chance of any other outcome for France but débâcle. But suppose he had accepted? That would not have changed the situation of France one whit, but it would have made all the difference to the selection of the options.

2

INTRODUCTION

by the Editor of the Thiers Papers

The precise role of Adolphe Thiers in the complete reversal of French policy during July and August 1870 was a mystery to all but a select few of his contemporaries, but now, a hundred years after his death, it is possible to reconstruct his activities during the crucial weeks. The centrepiece of the Thiers Centenary Exhibition in Paris in 1977 was a file of documents discovered the previous year during the demolition of offices in Aix-en-Provence which, it has been established, had formerly been occupied by a notary whose friendship with Thiers dated from their attending the law school there.

The documents have been translated and set out in chronological order below. They comprise excerpts from a diary, written in a small notebook; drafts and copies of letters; an original letter from General Trochu; and three cuttings from a German newspaper which strongly supported Bismarck's policies but which ceased to publish independently after his dismissal from office in 1890, and the files of which, therefore, have long since ceased to be available.

DIARY

Thursday, July 14. Crisis over. King of Prussia accepts our objections to having a scion of his house (even though only an 11th cousin!) on the throne of Spain. Leopold's father has withdrawn his son's candidature, 'firmly resolved not to let a minor family concern develop into a pretext for war'. Admirable sentiments! Ollivier[1] announces that peace is assured—which is as well, since our army is in no state to take on the Prussians.

Unfortunately our success will allow Gramont to crow over his getting the better of M de Bismarck (although I am confidentially informed that the Emperor himself contrived the whole business behind Gramont's back).

Lunched at the Café de la Paix with General Beaufort d'Hautpoul. Discussed Moltke,[2] with whom B d H served in Syria thirty years ago. Says Moltke knows beforehand exactly the results of a shock between two bodies at a certain angle— just like a great billiard player. Our own forces weakened by inept commanders; too many better at leading the cotillion than at leading troops—and promoted for that reason! High command riddled with personal rivalries—no grasp of the Prussian ideas of military science; in its present state, army would not suffer defeat, it would be destroyed.

In streets, popular agitation for war suddenly muted; assaults on foreigners ceased. General satisfaction at having put Prussia in her place. Press agitation also abates: it has been principally responsible for whipping up frenzy. It will be terrible if diplomacy ever is responsive to public opinion.

Dined at home with Eloise[3] and Mme Mère,[4] quieter in mind than for the last two weeks, since the announcement in the *Gazette de France.*

Gramont has only to tie up the loose ends, and even he cannot fail to do that properly.

Friday, July 15. I was wrong. Gramont has excelled himself. Not content with Leopold's withdrawal, he has now pressed for a guarantee by the King of Prussia that he would never again support a Hohenzollern candidature for the Spanish throne. The King has, it appears, refused (which Frenchman would have acted otherwise?). This is the quintessence of folly. The terms of the rejection, as given in the press, are designed to humiliate us, but as they were published in a special edition of Bismarck's *Norddeutsche Allgemeine Zeitung*, I would not be too certain that it represents accurately what the King of Prussia said.

Yesterday's rejoicing has turned into total fury. The universal

cry is for a march on Berlin, via Jena.[5] The centre of Paris is
congested with people from the faubourgs, anxious to chastise
the arrogance of the King of Prussia. They remind me of
lunatics whose keepers have absconded.

Chamber appalling! atmosphere of frenetic chauvinism:
deputies taking their cue from Biroteau who shouted that if
you are insulted you do not need to reflect. I asked Ollivier to
produce the depatches on which government policy was based.
He refused, on grounds that it would not conform to diplomatic
usages! Instead read out two telegrams from Benedetti[6]—which
I pointed out demonstrated that war was not necessary.
Ollivier countered by saying that the 'insult' which France had
to avenge lay not in the King of Prussia's refusal but in the fact
that it had been divulged throughout Europe: to support
which, he read out a report from a minor German newspaper
which he said was 'more or less accurate'. I asked the Ministry
if, with the substance of the quarrel settled in our favour, it was
willing to go to war over a mere matter of form. Catcalls,
sarcastic speculation about how many battalions I was worth
to the Prussians etc. Opposition insisted that disclosure of
documents be put to the vote! We got 84, against 159. The
Chamber adjourned to enable a commission on war credits to
be elected: Ollivier, Gramont, and Leboeuf[7] interrogated—
latter argued he must have a decision so as to mobilize ahead
of the Germans; 'the army was prepared down to the last
gaiter-button'. Gramont excused his late arrival on the grounds
that he had been with the Austrian ambassador and the Italian
minister and for that reason asked not to be pressed about
allies. The Commissioners reported themselves satisfied with
the government's explanations. The Chamber obediently voted
the credits—we mustered only ten votes against war.

On way home was assaulted by soldiers in Rue LaFayette—
wine, not politics. I am totally exhausted and cannot wait for
the prorogation.

Saturday, July 16. Overslept till nearly six; such strenuous trials
as yesterday are unsuited to my age. Journals raging for war,

congratulating Ministry on its valour, and the King of Prussia on my loyal service. Unable to settle to work: in mid-morning observed workman outside the house trying to stir up a demonstration by shouting that I had sold myself to the King of Prussia: the group dispersed when one solid bourgeois pointed out that the King had no need to buy me. Thereafter, all quiet— but it is as well that we are leaving for Trouville. Prudence as well as health demands a change of air.

EDITORIAL in
Klein-Kleckersdorfer Lokal-Anzeiger, July 16, 1870

M Thiers has given general satisfaction in Germany by his speech in the Corps Legislatif yesterday. In saying that the candidature of a Hohenzollern in Spain is no cause for war, he expresses the dominant opinions here. But M Thiers was in a minority in the French Chamber. The majority favour war— not over Spain but because they wish to halt the unification of Germany. They claim that our recent success in war against Denmark in 1864 and Austria in 1866 has made us into some kind of threat against them, and that they should therefore take steps against us at the earliest possible moment. Our French neighbours pride themselves on their logic but it is hardly logical to promote the unity of Italy and deny the same right to the peoples of Germany. M Thiers himself recognizes this, since his opposition hitherto has rested on traditional French ideas as to the balance of power. He has maintained that the organization of Germany in independent states is 'a fundamental principle of European politics'. The history of our country from the time of Richelieu until today proves only too conclusively that when a Frenchman uses these terms he intends that a weak because disunited Germany should exist as a campaigning ground for French armies. The memory of the chasseurs in the Duchy of Klein-Kleckersdorf is still vivid in the memory of our older inhabitants. Germany has suffered seventeen major invasions from across the Rhine in the last hundred and fifty years. Only a united Germany can put an end to them.

Yesterday, however, M Thiers modified his hostility sufficiently to rule out war. He may not be a friend of a united Germany but he has temporarily at least, ceased to be an enemy.

DIARY

Sunday, July 24. General Leboeuf on behalf of the Emperor offered me the Ministry of War! My immediate instinct was to refuse because I am 73 and feel exhausted by the last few days. Nevertheless, I temporized; asked Leboeuf whether he had resigned. He told me he wants an active command and was leaving for Metz. It occurred to me at that precise moment that 'an active command' was what I have myself wanted, and that this would be my last chance. I enquired what policy the Emperor wished me to implement, since I had not changed my opinion that war was totally unnecessary. Leboeuf remarked that he had no instructions. I thereupon returned the answer that I would be happy to assume office, if the policy required of me was consistent with my publicly expressed beliefs. He left. All I could think was that there might still be time to pull France back from the abyss—and that it was almost thirty years since I had held office.

Monday, July 25. My stipulation was accepted and the Emperor received me at St Cloud after dinner last night. I said bluntly that France needed peace and had declared war. The Emperor agreed, saying that my opposition to German unity would reassure Paris while my speech of July 15 would be a signal to all Europe that France was changing its policy. Could I bring about a peaceful outcome. I asked how much time we had. He replied wistfully that the Prussians had taken six weeks to mobilize in 1866. We agreed that people in the streets and some factions at Court (tactfully left unidentified) wanted war to wipe out a national humiliation, but that all we had with Prussia was a conflict of interest, which could be negotiated.

At that point, the Emperor collapsed on to a sofa, in severe pain. He told me what I did not know before, that four leading specialists had pronounced an operation for the removal of stones from his kidneys urgently necessary; that on his orders the Empress had not been informed, and that to reassure her, and the public, the latest bulletin on his health had been signed by only one surgeon. He (Napoleon) has asked for a second opinion from a famous English specialist, Mr Prescott-Hewitt. After his visit, he would decide. A servant was summoned to bring drops to relieve the pain, but he reappeared accompanied by the Empress and Gramont who immediately began to berate me about my 'pacifism' and 'defeatism', which imperilled Throne and Succession. War was the only argument those hateful Protestant Prussians understood: their chastisement would earn the Empire the gratitude of Europe.

I answered that we were undertaking a war in complete isolation, having accepted the odium of being the aggressor in the eyes of Europe, thus encouraging possible allies and sympathizers to remain aloof. They were aware, as possibly Gramont was not, that we actually had a pact of friendship with the state on which we had so improvidently declared war!

The Emperor sat silent—his eyes half-closed, concentrating more on his pain than on the discussion. (I wonder how often that has happened during the last two weeks.) It suddenly flashed through my mind that the Empress and Gramont did not realize that my appointment meant a complete reversal of policy. Should I make this explicit, or would that be going too far? They solved my problem by abruptly taking their leave.

The Emperor intuitively grasped my thoughts because he immediately observed, 'They do not really understand what I propose to do, with your help.' We were to act independently of all other authorities; I requested a document stating that I had full power to act, in case his attacks of pain should incapacitate him. He agreed, telling me to write it myself, for his signature.

I thereupon asked leave to withdraw; he looked exhausted.

This morning I arrived at the War Ministry; welcomed by chef de cabinet, expressing relief that I had taken over the direction of affairs. When I saw the sheaf of telegrams reporting the chaos of our mobilization, I could understand why; ordered concentration of army in main fortresses and camps. Metz, Belfort, Chalons. Wired changes to provincial garrisons, together with official confirmation of my appointment. Hope oath of loyalty will hold. Wired Trochu[8] to report immediately. Glanced at Stoffel's[9] reports from Berlin, which fully vindicate my stand; asked for Prefects' monthly reports on state of public opinion throughout France.

EDITORIAL in
Klein-Kleckersdorfer Lokal-Anzeiger, July 27, 1870.

It is reported from Paris that M Thiers has been appointed Minister of War, in place of General Leboeuf. Since his return to the Chamber of Deputies in 1863 M Thiers has been the acknowledged leader of the opposition groups to the policies of Kaiser Napoleon III. He has in recent months moderated his criticism, as the personal rule of Kaiser Napoleon has been modified into the present liberal regime in which the Emperor is more like a constitutional monarch.

It is obvious, from the treatment that he received on July 15, which we have already reported, that M Thiers commands the support of only a fraction in the Chamber of Deputies and that the Senate which voted the war credits on the same day with no dissentients, must be regarded as wholly hostile to him: under the new constitution, ministers are responsible to the Emperor but must be acceptable to the Corps Legislatif. M Thiers clearly is not. It is fortunate for him that the Corps Legislatif is in recess—a fact which perhaps explains the timing of his appointment.

(Our military correspondent comments on page 6).

Monsieur Thiers—War Minister

It is as unusual in France for a civilian to occupy the Ministry of War as it is here in Germany. M Thiers, however, has the military temperament. Destiny has not granted him a military career but is making some amends for the neglect of his potentialities for so long.

His support of the heretical views of General Trochu on the publication of the latter's book, *The French Army in 1867*, has alienated M Thiers from the Corps of General Officers of the Army of the Second Empire. It is reported, though not confirmed, that several senior commanders have already sent in their resignations. In any new appointments, it will be interesting to see whether General Trochu is recalled to a more important post than Commandant of the Pyrenees Military District. The higher echelons of the French Army are divided to a point at which the cohesion of its commanders becomes questionable.

These circumstances make M Thiers' appointment even more puzzling. He has not disowned his speech of July 15, but the government of which he is now a member has already declared war on Prussia, and the army is mobilizing. Does this portend a complete change of policy: if so, is M Thiers to lose the last vestiges of honour, or is France?

Alberich von und zu Klempner-Laden,
General der Infanterie a. D.

DIARY

Thursday, July 28. Long discussion with Trochu. He is adamant that any attacks across the Rhine would be disastrous; we have no allies in southern Germany, as we have had in the past, to create a diversion on the Prussian flank. Will try to get Trochu appointed Governor of Paris: meanwhile he is military adviser to me, a weaker position but not without its advantages since it does not have to be published.

Friday, July 29. Decided to close Place St Georges, sending Eloise and Mme Mère away, in case of trouble. Announcement of my appointment in the Journal Officiel brought denunciations from republican colleagues of my 'treachery' in taking office under the Emperor. Put in hand measures Trochu and I worked out. The bookseller near the Ministry has decorated his shop with an enormous strip of calico announcing that he has 'French-German dictionaries for the use of the French forces in Berlin'. Crowds still surging round streets: impromptu renderings of Marseillaise,[10] noise deafening. Learn that a man was badly beaten by a crowd outside the Café de Madrid in the Boulevard Montmartre for advocating peace, so sent Trochu new instructions. Fortunately, erecting barricades is more difficult than it was in '48. I never thought I should be grateful to that scoundrel Haussmann![11]

MEMORANDUM

The Problem of Extrication

(i) The kernel of the problem is that Bismarck wants war to complete the unification of Germany, which he has carried through with complete success north of the Main. Without this purpose, there is no point in his provoking France.

(ii) This specific purpose requires us to appear the aggressors (a role we have so far played to perfection!) so that the rulers of Bavaria and the other south German states can be shepherded into the Prussian fold.

(iii) The principal shepherd is Moltke, whose army, thanks to our rashness, is already mobilizing. It required six weeks in 1866 but how long now? Our generals stipulate four weeks as the very minimum. My own estimate, after reading Stoffel's reports, would be between two and three—which would have to be calculated from 16/17 July!

(iv) *Bismarck's specific purpose is a source of weakness in his strategy to the extent that it demands a particular response from us.*
Suppose we reject the role for which we have been cast? South Germany contains enough elements hostile to Bismarck to be welded into a coalition against Prussia, under Louis of Bavaria. But time is vital: once Prussia's army is in being, the South German states, unsupported by us or the Austrians, will have no option but to capitulate to Prussia and thus merge themselves in a united Germany.

(v) Since we cannot act positively ourselves, we must induce hesitation across the Rhine. Every postponement improves our chances of avoiding a war for which we are not prepared and of constructing a restraining force in the courts of Europe.

We must, therefore, *in spite of the fact that we have declared war*, so arrange our forces that the Prussians will find no *public* reason to cross the Rhine, or if they do, will look foolish or criminal in the eyes of Europe. We must announce that our troops will take up purely defensive positions well back from the Rhine: that any crossing of the frontier into Alsace or Lorraine will be completely unopposed: the Prussians can march to Paris if they like (what could they do if they got here?). The onus of aggression will then pass from us to them, if they care to accept it, but Bismarck knows he cannot bring in the South German states if Prussia takes the initiative. We can then bring in Britain to use her good offices, already offered: Austria and Russia will join in any arrangement which costs them nothing.

All these measures demand absolutely firm control at home. Here the problem centres on the Court and its cluster of Catholic 'ultras' and fire-eating officers. But the key is the Emperor himself: does anyone—he himself—know his mind? He cannot be guaranteed to hold to any one course, particularly in the presence of the Empress. The generals who support her can be dispersed to other commands or arrested, if need be, but she cannot.

The Court faction is strengthened by the streets— the danger is that some officers might be tempted to take charge of the agitation to restore the dictatorship and prosecute the war.

These contingencies suggest what has to be done.

The Emperor must be removed to hospital immediately.

I cannot do this:

The Empress must be told how serious the Emperor's condition is and be faced with the

someone will have to be found.
Philippe de Massa?[12]

gravity of the Prince Imperial's succeeding *now* at the age of 14, at the outset of a war which is by no means supported by all of France: only the Emperor can keep the Empire intact, but the Emperor's chances of survival diminish with every day's delay . . .
If she can be prevailed upon to live in the hospital, so much the better.

Gramont?

The Catholics must be appeased or at least distracted by our support for the Munich clericals (though it will require careful explanations in Florence).[13]

task for Trochu

Discipline must be imposed on the streets, but the measures will have to be coordinated with the preventive detention of any officers likely to side with the mob. If we control the army, the mob can do as it likes.

Everything depends on time.

Adolphe Thiers
July 29, 1870

It is ironical that my efforts to preserve France from impending catastrophe will help preserve the Empire. If we avoid war, my political and moral credit among the Opposition will be broken: if we are attacked, all the blame for the disaster will be shifted to me.

(*Editor's note:* Thiers' signature, the sentences appearing beneath it and the marginal comments are in his own hand: the rest was dictated.)

LETTER TO GENERAL TROCHU

(*Copy*)
29th July, 1870

Mon Général,

The disturbances in Paris are, in my judgement, reaching danger point—which may easily call for an immediate military response. The contingencies in which you should consider yourself free to proceed without further reference to me and in the knowledge of my full confidence, are

  (i) any attempt to seize the Emperor, the Royal Family, or Ministers (even M de Gramont!)
 (ii) any attempt to seize the Hotel de Ville for political purposes
(iii) Any attempt to seize a barracks or fortification or any part of the city which could be easily fortified or barricaded.

Otherwise, our policy must continue to be that the populace is allowed to circulate, to assemble and disperse, under the surveillance only of the police in the normal course of their duties. If however any of the three contingencies mentioned above should arise, then military action must be swift and thorough. We must not allow the regime to appear unable to assert its will. Force and justice are the only resources of society against the disorderly passions that foment among certain people.

DIARY

Sunday, August 1. Yesterday evening the King of Prussia arrived in Mayence to take command of the German forces. This indicates that their mobilization has gone much more smoothly than we had calculated. News of Emperor's condition released; he enters hospital tomorrow. Time is running out. German forces are concentrating in the area of Mayence-Trèves-Coblence though some units appear to be moving in the direction of the Sarre. Wired Leboeuf at Metz not to expect Emperor and remain in charge himself. The torrential rain is, from my point of view, a providential deterrent to marching and fighting.

But how to convey our intentions to the Prussians so that they will not mistake them? They will interpret the news of the Emperor as an additional opportunity for them to get into position. Effect of bulletin in Paris very satisfactory: opinion in the haute bougeoisie is already moving against the war: a thousand pities it was not articulated two weeks ago! Meanwhile we must try to sway the Press (whose present degree of freedom is due to my efforts!).

Discussed question of intervention by Britain with Lord Lyons[14] who came to express concern at the news about the Emperor. Lyons promises urgent representations in London and Windsor, and will cross tonight.

Saw Pietri[15]—to agree on measures for public order but slipped into the conversation the idea that Gramont might go to Munich himself to make direct contact with his friends, possibly en route for Rome. I cannot be sure he will rise to the bait—but it would get him out of the way on a pretext he can hardly refuse.

LETTER TO MINISTER OF THE INTERIOR

(Copy)
1st August, 1870

Dear Colleague,
As I recall, before the Empire took on its present liberal character, the government controlled the provincial Press through the distribution of contracts for printing orders for official notices and other publications. I presume this arrangement still exists; if I am correct it would provide

an excellent means of strengthening opinion in the provinces in favour of détente with Prussia. I would be grateful if you would urgently initiate some action to guide opinion in this direction.

Are there any Parisian newspapers which could be relied upon? I am particularly interested in *Le Petit Journal* which, as you know, is sold by a novel method through vendors directly on the street, instead of through subscriptions in the usual way.

With my highest respect,

LETTER FROM GENERAL TROCHU

Secret
1st August, 1870

My dear Thiers,

On my responsibility, I have in the last few days been in touch with certain officers whose favourable reception of my book led me to surmise that their view of our present situation would differ from that held by their commanding generals. They are, I need hardly add, all officers whose careers have been hampered by their intelligence and who might well have made a greater mark on their profession but for MacMahon's characteristically stupid prohibition.[16]

You will deduce that they were not difficult to convince that there are other ways of serving the Emperor and France than by going down to almost certain defeat, though I must insist they are patriotic and brave men, who will do their duty whatever form it may take. They have agreed that they will hold themselves ready to carry out any orders which I may give them in the Emperor's name, on condition that I give them in person and to all at the same time.

This decision is understood by all to be provisional until ratified by 'the highest authority'. That done, I would then take steps to have the individual officers transferred to the capital where they can all come under my jurisdiction, so that they can deal with *any* contingency at once. May I request your authorization to proceed? They will understand that notification of re-posting means that permission has been granted. They will not know by whom. I have no copy of this letter which I am sending by my batman.

> With my highest esteem
> signed
> *Trochu*

DIARY

August 2. Discovered that Count von Solms, chargé in the Prussian Ambassador's absence, had not yet completed the formalities for closing down the embassy, so asked him to call on me, offering escort to protect him from the mob. He elected to come in a closed carriage. Showed him my written authority from the Emperor as justifying my right to expound our new policy. Explained my personal position by saying that, although I had been opposed to German unification, the time for French intervention was four years ago on the side of Austria, not now. I admired Count Bismarck as a realist and hoped he entertained the same opinion of me; realistically considered, there were no problems between Prussia and France which could not be negotiated. My appointment was itself evidence that the Emperor shared this view. Gramont no longer expressed the policy of France.

Von Solms then asked, 'What about the declaration of war?' adding that the law and customs of relations between princes did not allow such a declaration to be withdrawn. I agreed but assured him that we were not going to proceed with the conventional military arrangements following such a declaration.

The Earl of Shelburne

Benjamin Franklin

Benito Juarez   (*Radio Times Hulton Picture Library*)

Adolphe Thiers   (*Mansell Collection*)

Our mobilization could not be stopped, but its direction would be changed; the troops would be concentrated in the existing forts and camps, to demonstrate to all the world that we had no intention of invading Germany. I had given instructions that the major powers of Europe and the courts of southern Germany be informed of the fact. Von Solms incredulous. He was intelligent enough to grasp that Prussia would now have to assume the role of aggressor but was totally unprepared to think further since what I was saying transgressed all his ideas of honourable behaviour. I went on to say that, of course, if Prussia insisted on invading France, a new situation would be created: there had been no time to settle with the Emperor on our response to that eventuality, but my own opinion was that any Prussian attack should be entirely unopposed. They could march to Paris if they wished and we would welcome Counts Bismarck and Moltke just as we had in 1867 at the Great Exhibition; we might even revive *The Grand Duchess of Gerolstein* which they enjoyed so much, or get M Offenbach to compose another piece specially in their honour. It would be particularly fitting, since he was born in Germany and worked in France.

Von Solms looked very upset. He said my proposals were totally unprecedented and would cause chaos. I asked if he thought war would produce any less chaos, reminding him that, only two weeks ago, Britain had offered to mediate and that Bismarck had not rejected it, leaving that to us; he could not consistently reject it now, when French policy had changed. We preferred bilateral negotiations since, as he (Solms) well knew, the more parties to negotiations the less likely any one of them is to get what he wants. But we would not flinch from discussions between all the interested parties on the problems of the entire Rhineland, from Holland down to Switzerland. Before any negotiations, it would be essential that the King of Prussia and the Emperor meet—which would depend on the King's willingness and the Emperor's health. Once the principles had been established, we, the servants, could be entrusted with negotiating the details.

Von Solms enquired what guarantees could I offer that this policy would not also be reversed as suddenly and radically as the last. France *had* declared war on Prussia. I accepted the point but remarked that throughout history (of which he knew I had made some study) the object of declaring war was to secure peace. The fighting merely settled the terms on which peace was secured and for how long. As for guarantees, we could no doubt arrange to have Prussian garrisons in the Rhineland or even partition Belgium, as the Emperor and Bismarck had discussed at Biarritz in 1865. France would be prepared to make ample concessions to the Prussian point of view.

But we had not unlimited time. The armies were mobilizing; no one could be certain of the outcome of the Emperor's operation. I asked him to report my views directly to the King of Prussia and promised to keep myself available to go to Mayence fully empowered to make pledges and enter into engagements on the Emperor's behalf.

Von Solms left with a special laisser passer and an escort of dragoons with instructions from me to cut their way through any attempted resistance. Our interview lasted an hour—one can only hope. But it is better to try to arrest the torrent, even without hope of succeeding.

Editor's Note

As all the world knows, Thiers went to Mayence, incognito, and opened negotiations having forewarned the South German states, which, led by Ludwig II of Bavaria, denounced their military conventions with Prussia and withdrew their support of Prussian policy. Moltke urged the invasion of France notwithstanding but was opposed by Bismarck and the King, who personally was not anxious to preside over another war. On 2 September, William I and Napoleon III met at Sedan and agreed on the terms of a settlement of outstanding Rhineland problems. The German forces returned to their depots and eventually demobilized—with France defraying the mobilization costs, under an indemnity agreement. Contingents were left along the Rhine and some departments of France were temporarily garrisoned by Prussian forces. The British offer of good offices was accepted but the crisis was resolved bilaterally: both France and Prussia renewed their guarantee of the neutrality of Belgium as part of the general Rhineland settlement arrived at by the Conference of Brussels, 1871. Bismarck attempted to resign and retire to his estates at Varzin but was dissuaded by the King. Moltke retreated into silence. Count von Solms appears to have left no record of his mission.

Sections of the population of Paris, as Thiers expected, revolted against the concessions which the French government had necessarily made as part of the settlement. The insurgents attempted to set up an alternative regime, the Commune (March—May 1871). Thiers withdrew all government forces from the capital and organized its recapture. The rising was put down with the utmost ferocity. An obscure German socialist, living in London, published a pamphlet about the episode, which attained some subsequent notoriety.* The distinction which Thiers drew between declaring war and the action of war has become a commonplace of international law though still disputed by traditionalists.†

3

The victory of Prussia in 1870 put an end to the primacy France had exercised in Europe for over two hundred years, which Frenchmen had come to regard as the natural due of

---

*See K. H. Marx, *The Civil War in France* (London, 1871).
†See Wonnebald Weissnichtwasser, *'Krieg oder Frieden'* oder *'Frieden oder Krieg'? Beitrag zum Versuch einer kritischen Einführung in die theoretische Entwicklung eines Konzepts*, Posen am Rhein, 1896.

their superior civilization. (In this respect, the débâcle was even more traumatic than that of 1940.)

But in mid-1870, neither the war nor the subsequent Prussian victory were inevitable. Take the assumption, shared by most Frenchmen including Thiers, that Bismarck was the final arbiter of Prussian policy: in fact, that role belonged to the King, William I, who was not accustomed simply to ratifying his Chancellor's policy judgements. In July 1870, William was so averse to war that Bismarck was on the verge of retiring to his estates. The war credits vote in Paris changed their minds. Nevertheless, until he took formal control of the army at Mainz on July 31, William was a reluctant warrior, open to any initiative for peace.

This disposition reflected not just a genuine desire to avoid another war in his old age, but also a wholesome respect for French military prowess. The incompetence of the French command was only demonstrated from August onwards; in July, the army was thought to be a formidable fighting machine, which its new weapons, the mitrailleuse and the chassepôt rifle, had given a keener cutting edge. The French army was therefore still a weighty factor in any alliance or policy of deterrence and could lend strength to any diplomatic initiatives aimed at the widespread anti-Prussian opinion in south Germany.

Twice during the crisis, Britain offered to mediate: the second time, on the eve of hostilities. Bismarck did not expressly reject mediation, leaving that to the French, 'proof' of whose aggression was essential to his plans. He necessarily risked leaving France an option. The option was exercised: on the evening of July 14, the cabinet decided in favour of international mediation: within the hour, it reversed its decision on the (false) assumption that Austria would intervene against Prussia.

One should remember, too, that Napoleon had for some years followed an alternative policy, of coming to an arrangement, perhaps even an alliance, with Prussia, in which their mutual difficulties could be solved, most probably at the expense of Belgium. Negotiations had gone far enough to provide a vehicle for accommodation in July 1870.

All these advantages were thrown away in the Gadarene rush into war, between July 15 and 19. Thiers unceasingly insisted on the need for time—even twenty-four hours—for a peaceful solution, but time was recklessly jettisoned by the French government, along with its other advantages. After the declaration of war, the only time of which France disposed was the period between the mobilization of forces and their concentration for battle. It was not much—about twenty days—but enough for an energetic and peace-minded minister to put together the lineaments of an alternative to fighting. A peace initiative would, at worst, have won France the sympathy of non-committed states and thus allowed the politics of the war to develop in her favour, while, at best, it would have conduced to a negotiated resolution of the dispute. With Napoleon sick, only Thiers had the resolution, the experience and the moral authority to press through the necessary measures. Had he done so, '1870' might not have been the precursor of '1914' or '1939'.

NOTES

1 Emile Ollivier (1825–1913), Liberal lawyer, Prime Minister of France in 1870.

2 Helmuth von Moltke (1800–91), chief of the Prussian General Staff.

3 Madame Thiers, née Dosné, married Thiers in September 1833, aged 16.

4 Madame Euridice Dosné, wife of Lille banker and industrialist; opened a salon in Faubourg St Germain; from 1822 political patroness of Thiers.

5 Jena: in Saxony, scene of French victory over Prussia, October 14, 1806.

6 French Ambassador to Prussia.

7 General and Minister of War.

8 Louis Trochu (1815–96), General, author of *L'armée française en 1867* —an attack on the legends of the French army and its organization and tactics.

9 Baron Eugene Georges Stoffel, French Military Attaché in Berlin whose reports (subsequently published) provided accurate information about the Prussian army and penetrating insight into its effectiveness.

10 The *Marseillaise* was banned under the Empire.

11 Baron Georges Haussmann, Prefect of the Seine from 1853; in charge of the redevelopment of Paris; resigned in January 1870 under pressure from Ollivier, after inquiries into his handling of the project's finances.

12 Philippe de Massa, cavalry officer used by Thiers on July 11, 1870 as intermediary with Emperor over crisis developments.

13 Florence was the capital of Italy, united in 1859–60 through French policy but with the exception of the city of Rome where the Pope ruled supported by a French garrison whose continued presence was demanded by the Clerical party at St Cloud. In July 1870, some leading figures in French politics thought this more important than the Prussian problem.

14 Lord Lyons, British Ambassador in Paris, 1867–87.

15 Joachim Pietri, Prefect of Police.

16 'I eliminate from the list of promotions any officer whose name I have read on a cover of a book'—Marshal MacMahon.

If I had been . . .

WILLIAM EWART GLADSTONE IN 1880

'How I would have solved the Irish problem.'

OWEN DUDLEY EDWARDS

1

Broadly speaking, there were two traditions of British policy towards Ireland throughout the nineteenth century: the Whig tradition, which under Irish pressure made some concessions to legislative reform, and the Peelite tradition, which was more prepared to consider genuine social remedies. Gladstone, who had been a follower of Peel, and who ultimately joined many Whigs in the new Liberal party, inherited both of these legacies when he came to power as Prime Minister for the first time. He also inherited the British governmental readiness to suspend habeas corpus *and bring in coercive legislation at any sign of disorder. In his first administration he introduced several reforms including the disestablishment of the Protestant episcopalian Church of Ireland (third largest Irish religious sect in numbers) and a Land Act that established the principle of government intervention between landlord and tenant.*

Gladstone was convinced that he had solved the Irish land question, although in fact his Act had done nothing to restrain the awesome power of the Irish landlords, few of whom were 'improvers' after the English pattern. After an unsuccessful effort at Irish university reform, Gladstone fell from power in 1874 and retired from politics. Despite his visit to Ireland in 1877, he seems to have retained no further interest in the place. Meanwhile Disraeli's government offered repression, but nothing else, and when harvests began to fail in bad weather conditions of 1877, and American competition revived heavily, the Irish crisis began to mount. Isaac Butt's Home Rule party in the House of Commons grew more vigorous, and certain of its members began to associate themselves with a powerful popular land agitation, in Ireland and in America, the most notable such figure being Charles Stewart Parnell. Distress, evictions and agitation reached alarming heights in 1879. An Irish Land League was founded under Parnell's Presidency and he sailed to raise money and support in North America where he campaigned very extensively in the first months of 1880. Meanwhile Disraeli scented a crisis and interpreted it as requiring vigorous measures of repression: he called an election on that. Gladstone, returning to politics with his famous Midlothian campaign, showed himself, at the age of 70, as forceful and successful a popular agitator as Parnell was proving to be.

The Liberals were returned to power with Gladstone as Prime Minister. Parnell was elected leader of the Home Rule party in the Commons. He and his followers remained in opposition (although the defeated minority of the party came to sit with the Liberals) and were almost entirely preoccupied with the mounting agrarian crisis in Ireland.

It would have been easy to assume in 1880 that the Irish problem would always be insoluble: but that is not what Gladstone did. He came much closer to assuming he had solved it. What was even odder was that Gladstone, back in Parliament, seemed oblivious of the new wave of democratic sentiment upon which he had so powerfully capitalized in his Midlothian campaign. Both Britain and Ireland—for different reasons—were sending signals demanding a radical government with radical measures: Gladstone gave them a Whig-aristocratic one. Instead, therefore, of addressing himself to the Irish crisis, Gladstone allowed himself to be overtaken by it. He introduced remedial measures in a highly confused Land Act of 1881, followed by an Arrears Act of 1882; he also imprisoned Parnell and his leading followers in 1881, and released them in 1882. Then Parnell's enemies assassinated the Liberal Chief Secretary for Ireland, Lord Frederick Cavendish (who had just replaced W. E. Forster). In fact, Parnell —as the sequel to his imprisonment showed—had been a means of

restraining violence rather than of increasing it. In retrospect,
the lapse of a year may seem little: at this particular time, it was
far too much. But suppose Gladstone had displayed greater
imagination in 1880, before the spiral of distrust, recrimination,
violence and death had begun to mount . . .

2

I was not alone in my sense of the popular stirrings. But my
opponents responded to it with the tricks of the demogogue
with which, to put no fine point on it, Mr Disraeli (now
ennobled to the Earldom of Beaconsfield) had animated his
late Ministry; and the Irish agitator, Mr Parnell, for all of his
youth, was proving himself a virtuoso leader of the mob in
Ireland and in North America. The better to guard themselves
against such men, the people needed and must have sound,
enlightened and far-sighted leadership.

In characterizing the conduct of my opponents as demago-
guery, I drew a sharp distinction between their messages. With
Lord Beaconsfield's false coin of Empire I would have nothing
to do; I repudiated it, very notably at Midlothian in the course
of the elections of 1880, by offering the genuine specie of
invitation to the populace to participate in political activity,
my terms being at once moral and educative, as indicating to
the lower orders their rights and their duties in political life.
Furthermore, Lord Beaconsfield went to the country by means
of a public letter to the Duke of Marlborough, his Irish Viceroy,
a letter which I do not hesitate to term inflammatory, his
manifest intention being to convulse the public with fear as to
the designs of Irishmen. But I conceded that Mr Parnell's
appeal rested on a true social crisis. His proceedings in North
America had at least furthered the generous stirrings of the
American philanthropic purse which even now were all that
stood between Ireland and Famine—galling as it might be that

he had also sought to make the Americans the moral arbiters in a case he presented as one of British injustice. I at least would answer that, and by deeds as well as by words.

The opportunity to do so became mine when it fell to me to form my second government in 1880. From the outset, I refused to consider a cabinet that failed to reflect the new progressive spirit of the times. Noblemen had to show just cause for consideration: thus, when it was said that the fifth Marquis of Lansdowne should be considered for a place, I demurred. That he was possessed of talents, I granted; but I questioned that his claims for consideration outweighed those of men of lesser rank but of greater political flexibility, experience and achievements. With deeper sentiments of personal regret I also set my face against the inclusion of the Duke of Argyll in the cabinet. His Grace had honoured me by his personal friendship, but I was mindful of his resignation from my first cabinet on the very mild measures which I embodied in the Irish Land Act of 1870. It would clearly be impossible to obtain his support for any more radical step such as the times warranted. No good purpose could be served by the offer of a cabinet post to men, however eminent or talented, who would embarrass the government by resignation at a time when the fairest of auspices would be needed for the introduction of necessary measures of land reform.

I certainly declined to countenance any proscription of peers from places in government which emanated from the vulgar principle of hostility to the noble orders: that would be as cardinal a folly as their inclusion for reasons of rank alone. My measures would need friends in the House of Lords. Happily, I had men of proven loyalty and a nice judgement as to the concessions which had to be made by the dictates of circumstance—men like Lord Granville, whose beautiful and generous nature bade fair to make him well loved in a land where many of his countrymen were not. He was offered, and accepted, the Irish Viceregal Lodge.

But most of my cabinet came from the House of Commons and its radical elements were given full representation. Specifically, I made Mr Chamberlain Chancellor of the Exchequer, an office that my age and cares prevented me from occupying concurrently with leading the government. Mr Chamberlain knew his figures. The Queen protested, as did many members of the House of Lords, but the country accepted radicals like Mr Chamberlain as an earnest of future legislation in the furtherance of its claims.

When Parliament had met, had affirmed its lack of faith in the administration of Lord Beaconsfield, and had approved my Ministry, I took an early opportunity of meeting with Mr Parnell. I was impressed with his curious restraint in private and his lack of Hibernian loquacity. From my minute of the conversation I can set it forth in something close to its true form. I began by asking him what measures he advocated to meet the needs of the present Irish situation. I advised him not to speak of any measure of Home Rule, a demand neither rational nor acceptable at this time.

P: A peasant proprietorship.

G: How achieved?

P: The government must purchase the estates and then sell them to the tenantry.

G: But the Irish tenants have no money.

P: Then lend it to them on the most indefinite terms.

G: This is revolution . . .

P: It has the precedent of the land purchase clause in your own Land Act of 1870.

I reminded Mr Parnell that his late leader, Mr Isaac Butt,[1] only called for the fixity of tenure, a fair rent and the right of free sale of the goodwill of the holding by the tenant. 'These things are needed now, but they solve nothing,' was his rejoinder. I remarked that should I introduce a scheme of the kind he was now proposing, I might not control a majority of the votes in the House of Commons.

P: With our votes, you do.

G: And if I do not introduce such a measure, you persist in obstructing the business of government?

He observed, almost with an air of indifference, that it was not impossible. I replied with some heat that I did not care to deal with threats. 'You abhorred the violence of the Fenians,'[2] replied Mr Parnell, 'but you introduced legislation in your last government to remedy Irish grievances of which they were a manifestation.'

I asked Mr Parnell, did he believe there would be more violence?

P: There already is.

G: In support of you?

P: It threatens my authority.

G: Some of your followers use very violent language.

P: They are excitable. I control their excitement.

G: You are committed to constitutional means?

P: My talents do not lie in the use of other means.

G: If it is a question of winning Irish faith in constitutional means rather than in the encouragement of recourse to anarchy and rapine, Mr Parnell, I will stand your friend.

It was a strong statement, but, within those limits and no further, it was no more than I believed.

That was my singular interview with Mr Parnell. I confess that it left a powerful effect upon my mind. His quiet, precise fashion of speech bred a conviction of sincerity which a man of greater oratorical talents could not produce. And events quickly bore out the shrewdness of his observation and deductions.

I took an early opportunity of requesting Sir Charles Dilke,[3] my new Chief Secretary for Ireland, to visit the worst districts in Mayo, Kerry and Donegal. The enormous publicity and particular information given by the newspapers, especially the American prints, made it possible for him to rely on more than police reports in the assessments he despatched to me several times during each week.

In addition, I conversed with men in my party who knew Ireland, giving particular attention to those who had acquaintance with the antecedents or the present course of the crisis. I also spoke with members of Mr Parnell's party. I was struck by one difference in all of them from him: they talked more, and said less. They had a knowledge which was not his, but they lacked his hold on every aspect of the situation.

Disorder in Ireland grew worse. Crowds rallied to Mr Parnell's meetings in a manner reminiscent to me of my late campaign in Midlothian; the grim spectre of famine still darkened the sky; and much though I deplored the methods of Mr Parnell's agrarian following, such as the 'boycott',[4] I acknowledged that it at least offered an alternative to violence against persons. I have naturally preserved a minute of a conversation on the subject which was accorded to me by the Queen.

She began by terming Mr Parnell's movement 'wholly communistic'. I sought to expound to her the fact that, since it was founded on a desire for the acquisition of property, it carried with it a respect for the principle of property.

'I cannot,' she said, 'permit legislation which rewards crime and outrage.'

The Queen was hostile to any concession to Mr Parnell, but I knew that I must have her goodwill if I was to honour my undertakings to him.

'Your Majesty might wish,' I observed, 'to make a state visit to County Mayo, where the social conditions which have given rise to crime and outrage are exhibited at their worst. The conditions in which these unfortunate men and women live could not fail to move Your Majesty's generous sensibilities.'

'Such an arduous undertaking might lead the people to conclude with indignation that I countenance the infamous proceedings of Parnell and his creatures.'

'The public,' I countered, 'would, on the contrary, be moved by the evident earnestness with which Your Majesty patently wished to acquaint yourself with the problems that exist in Ireland and with ways of relieving the unhappiness in that afflicted corner of your realm. A ruler of less personal courage,' I added, 'might shrink from such a journey.'

'Do you accuse your Sovereign of lack of courage?' she demanded.

'Not in the last, Madam,' I declared with solemnity. 'I know that Your Majesty will prove an example to all your subjects in resolution and fortitude. The good effects of Your Majesty's visit to Ireland after the awful famine of the 1840s were incalculable. It is true that Ireland may be more perilous to visit now than it was then.'

She retorted with true spirit: 'We are not afraid!'

Of course she did not wish to go, and of course I did not wish her to go. The likelihood of a violent attempt upon her life was too great, and the consequent revulsion of public feeling in Britain too certain. I could not venture to presume unduly on Mr Parnell's control over the violent elements remaining as strong as it was, and even now he was clearly unable to prevent many outrages from being committed. He had stated himself that he had enemies who would rejoice in the collapse of his power, especially when presented with a prospect at once so gratifying to them and so hideous to the British public as the assassination of the Queen.

Yet my observations did make the Queen in a sense my colleague in my mission to pacify Ireland. My own decision to visit Mayo strengthened her conviction in that regard. What I saw confirmed my belief in the tragic reality behind Mr Parnell's agitation.

Therefore, towards the closing months of 1880, I brought forward a new Land Bill, giving the fullest possible governmental assistance to tenant purchase of land holdings. I was advised that the Lords would throw it out. I said that, if so, I would ask the Queen to dissolve Parliament, a proceeding to which neither her old hostility nor her new hopes would be adverse. I made it a very simple Bill to remove any ambiguities which might invite further difficulties. The Lords signalled their intention to rebel.

I said a word to Mr Labouchere[5] before a meeting in Northampton at which we were both to speak, and in his speech he declared the necessity for a measure to curb the powers of the Lords. I made no reference to his proposal in my own observations from the platform but expressed my own admiration for him in terms which were, perhaps, somewhat excessive. (It was certainly by no wish of mine that he compared the mental processes of their Lordships to the ratiocinative powers of the common parrot, to the bird's advantage.)

The Queen showed some signs of her earlier alarm, but was mollified by my assurance that my intentions were to prevent the need for any such change. I was therefore enabled to advise their Lordships, on Her Majesty's reluctant authority, that a prompt creation of peers would follow any attempt to reject the legislation. I added that the terms proposed were far more likely to benefit the landlord interest than would a much more injurious measure, perhaps omitting compensation, such as in my opinion must inevitably follow a long and wasteful agrarian struggle from which both parties would suffer irremediably. In the event, our majority in the Lords was to include many members of the Conservative party who proved highly sympathetic to this view of the land question. Their numbers were more than sufficient to outweigh any adverse influence occasioned by the defection from Liberal ranks of the Duke of Argyll and the Marquis of Lansdowne. The Bill was passed, and the future prosperity of Ireland may be said to have dated from that moment.

Mr Parnell's personal influence suffered somewhat at the next election, but many of his more notable followers did well. We did not as yet endeavour to detach them with tenders of office, but we found a sensible diminution in their acrimony or, in the case of the more vociferous of their number, a satisfactory direction of it against the Conservatives. In the mean time, our hold on the votes of the Irish now domiciled in Britain was assured. Mr Parnell himself was glad to accept the post of Governor-General of Canada when it fell vacant in the course of my third administration, with the title of first Earl of Avondale; the considerations of his private life, of which political surveillance had made me fully aware, enhanced the need for its acceptance . . .

3

Some twenty years ago Vladimir Nabokov's *Lolita* was published in Britain amid furious controversy, and Kingsley Martin, *The New Statesman*'s greatest editor, finished his 'London Diary' of the week with the words:

'Well,' said I, on reading *Lolita*, 'if I were George Weidenfeld, I wouldn't publish that book.'

'Ah,' said my friend, 'but if you were George Weidenfeld, you would.'

If I had been Gladstone in 1880, the government would probably have fallen within a month and the Prime Minister led away to some quiet retreat. And if Mr Gladstone were me, I think it fair to say that my own family and university colleagues might find the old man even more tiresome to live with than they find me. So we have to limit the scope of this imaginative operation. On the one hand, I have tried not to endow Gladstone with the mental processes of a Socialist Catholic Irishman living in Edinburgh almost a century later; on the other, I could have had no hope of producing an alternative policy for Gladstone if he were to remain irredeemably circumscribed by his own outlook and the social and political attitudes of 1880.

Thus, I had to capitalize on those of Gladstone's characteristics that might have led him towards the flexibility that I have invented—such as his astute capacity to assess his younger colleagues. Most of Gladstone's contemporaries, for instance, seem to have had a vastly inflated view of Joe Chamberlain, particularly when they were hostile to him. In 1880 many conservatives in both Tory and Liberal ranks seem genuinely to have regarded the Birmingham industrialist and former Mayor as a potential harbinger of social revolution. After the Home Rule crisis of 1886 Parnell termed him 'the man who killed Home Rule'. The publication of Chamberlain's own political memoir in the mid-twentieth century revealed to those who had eyes to see that Chamberlain was in fact a man of remarkably petty mind, perpetually cost-accounting trifles of personal diplomacy to his own advantage. Gladstone has been criticized for clipping the wings of Chamberlain's ambition, and there is a case for this criticism. But the assumptions on which he seems to have done so seem in part to have been based on an estimate of Chamberlain's character and moral worth which was in fact shrewder than those of his juniors.

For all of his high-souled rhetoric, Gladstone had built up by 1880 an extraordinary political dexterity in a political career spanning half a century. Labouchere's famous insight that he didn't object to the Old Man always having the ace of trumps up his sleeve but did resent his insistence that God Almighty put it there, should not be seen as an indication of any particular tension between the extreme moralism of Gladstone's political utterances and the legerdemain by which he regulated the niceties of intra- and inter-party conflicts. He had developed political attitudes and ambitions by his later years in which his genuine examinations of conscience and his pragmatic political sense were well meshed. And I have tried to attribute to my fictional Gladstone the mind and nature of the factual one. He had by 1880, acquired great breadth of vision, actual and potential; his energy for a man in his seventies was incredible; and his life was graded and ordered far beyond that of any of his fellows. If this essay makes demands on his perception, it is important to note that he was anything but casual in his attention to business, even in the reading of fan-letters. He punctiliously dated letters whose writers had omitted that duty, and he filed away personal archives whose magnitude is simply stupendous. Thus, the invention above represents not only what he *could* have done, or what he could have *done*, but also what *he* could have done. And to some extent, of course, what he actually did. But the time has come to separate fact from fiction.

Disraeli (who *was* ennobled to the Earldom of Beaconsfield) *did* call the election of 1880 on an Irish scare issue and the press at the time *did* argue that famine and chaos loomed in Ireland. Gladstone's Midlothian campaign *did* use participation politics and popular appeal as never before witnessed in Britain, although matched by Parnell in Ireland and in America (and anticipated by Daniel O'Connell, notably in 1843). Further-more, the Liberals *did* win the election and Gladstone *was* right in thinking that he had a mandate for radical reform, particularly on the Irish question. But he *did not* choose a cabinet responsive to the progressive mood in the country and, instead, lumbered his administration with a plethora of aristo-crats, of whom Lord Lansdowne ratted on him over a very mild measure of compensation for evicted tenants in 1880, and the Duke of Argyll over his Land Act of 1881.

Far from making Joseph Chamberlain his Chancellor of the Exchequer, Gladstone *never* gave Chamberlain major cabinet office at any point and thereby alienated him; indeed, unlike my fictional Gladstone, the real one limited his own effectiveness and area of perceptiveness by insisting on making himself Chancellor (as he had done before) as well as Prime Minister. Then again, Gladstone *did not* show any sign of seeing an Irish crisis when he came into office, and must thereby have been one of the very few men in the English-speaking world to remain ignorant of it. He *did not* show any awareness of Parnell's achievement in the USA in January and February of 1880. He *did not*, indeed, have a sense of Parnell's achievement in agita-tion at all until it was forced upon him. He *did not* try to get to terms with Parnell until April 1882, having previously im-prisoned him (after which violence became much worse). He *did not* pay any substantial attention to minor Parnellites and Liberal figures who knew Ireland well (beyond occasional notice of good speeches in the House of Commons). Gladstone *did* bring in a radical measure in the Land Act of 1881, but he *did not* take up the solution of Land Purchase, confining himself to Isaac Butt's old aims of fixity of tenure, fair rent, and the right of free sale of the goodwill of the holding by the tenant. He *did* have a radical Chief Secretary (in W. E. Forster) but he *did not* listen to Forster's more radical proposals, while Forster, for his part, showed none of the perceptiveness of radicals of the younger generation such as Sir Charles Dilke.

Gladstone *did not* advocate a Royal visit to Ireland although

Victoria did actually go there in 1895 and 1900 (Gladstone himself went in 1877 when conditions were good, but never returned). *Nor* did Gladstone carry his diplomacy with Victoria further than lecturing her, although she had been radically altered in her political attitudes by Melbourne, Prince Albert and Disraeli, successively, and might have been again. Forster *did* at one point offer a very indirect threat to the Lords; Gladstone *did not* try to confront them, at any point, even when in 1893 they undid his work of the previous eight years by throwing out the Second Home Rule Bill passed by the House of Commons.

I have tried to play this game fairly to Gladstone, ascribing solutions to him consistent with his own situation and interests as well as those of Ireland. The question of the wishes and expectations of the British electorate in 1880 is vital to this Irish matter: we may choose to assume that the British voter was little moved by the Irish famine (and we might be wrong), but the Irish voter in Britain, then and later, was a vital factor to be taken into consideration. When Parnell put up T. P. O'Connor for the Scotland division of Liverpool in 1885 (a seat O'Connor won and held for some forty years), he brought into the open an electoral danger to which the Liberals should have been alive much earlier. But to consolidate a Liberal hold over Irish votes in Britain, Home Rule did not need to be the answer. It might have lost much of its force in the event of a quick solution of the land question by a government showing itself responsive to just social demands. Gladstone needed to make the Union appear a real partnership rather than the administrative convenience which it had previously been presented as, and a radical programme in Ireland would win electoral returns from Irish and British voters, even if it was the radicalism rather than the Hibernian aspect of the operation which the British masses would welcome.

I could have offered a different solution: a really drastic measure of Home Rule in 1880, leaving the Irish to work out their own land question. It would have gone through before conservative Unionism had been consolidated and hardened in

Ulster. But I don't think this is on the cards for Gladstone in 1880. He had a mandate then for radicalism, including land reform, but not for Home Rule. The evidence he could have obtained in 1880 testified to the need for land reform; a leap of faith would have been needed then for Home Rule.

On a long-term level, my solution is not a prophylactic against the Easter Rising of 1916 which, after all, followed years of extremely good government of the middle classes, if not of the urban workers. But the delay in land reform increased a social propensity to violence in Ireland. The methods of the land war, such as the boycott, legitimized social ostracism and led to exclusive dealing, ultimately on a religious sectarian level. The land war was not sectarian, but its prolongation awoke sectarian fires. Ulster Protestantism became alarmed when the question moved from social terms, with which many of its votaries sympathized, to national terms, which seemed to threaten cultural suffocation. And then the roots of the present crisis were in active formation.

But if it had happened as I suggested, and Parnell had become a has-been, would the great cultural energy which his movement ultimately stirred up, have taken place? Would there have been an Irish Renaissance? Would the genius of the young Yeats have been kindled into flame without the background of nationalist excitement? Would Henry George never have come to the British Isles and hence have failed to send Bernard Shaw on the road to Socialism? Would Oscar Wilde have settled for being a social climber rather than a social rebel? And would the Joyce family have eaten their Christmas dinner in peace, with no anti-clerical challenges to the conformity of their hopeful son James who would accordingly go on, untroubled, to become a Jesuit priest noted for the enthusiasm and artistry he brought to the business of teaching the *Odyssey* to the senior classes in Greek in Belvedere College, Dublin?

All of which, I hope, shows the overwhelming importance of what Mr Gladstone did, or did not do, in 1880.

NOTES

1 Isaac Butt (1813–79), leader of the Irish Home Rulers in the House of Commons, 1871–9.

2 Fenians: an Irish secret society which perpetrated a fiasco of an insurrection in 1867 followed by outrages in England.

3 Sir Charles Dilke (1843–1911), Radical Liberal Member of Parliament whom Gladstone in fact made Undersecretary of State for Foreign Affairs in 1880.

4 Captain Charles S. Boycott was an English army officer who, as local agent for an absentee landowner, refused to accept lower rents than those to which his employer was legally entitled. As a result, he was faced with total ostracism, and his name entered the vocabulary.

5 Henry Du Pré Labouchere (1831–1912), journalist, wit and Radical Liberal Member of Parliament for Northampton at the time.

If I had been . . .

ALEXANDER KERENSKY IN 1917

'How I would have prevented the Bolshevik Revolution.'

HAROLD SHUKMAN

1

In the late nineteenth century, tsarist Russia was in a ferment of political frustration. In 1881, Tsar Alexander II was assassinated and the next few years saw the brutal repression of any form of political liberalism, real or imagined. Early in the twentieth century, the country was defeated in war by its Eastern rival Japan, and shortly afterwards, in 1905, a revolution nearly brought an end to the centuries-old Romanov regime. Tsar Nicholas II was only able to maintain his authority by agreeing to set up a form of representative assembly, the 'Duma'. Nothing fundamental was changed by the establishment of the Duma and when Russia found itself at war again in 1914, this time with Germany, all the old revolutionary discontent looked like breaking out again. Russia did poorly in the war and the remote and incompetent regime was again subjected to great pressure. This time the pressure was intolerable.

The Tsar abdicated in March 1917 and his place was taken by a Provisional Government in which a leading figure—later the leading figure—was Alexander Kerensky. At the same time, city-based committees of workers and soldiers (known as 'soviets') sprang up in the capital, Petrograd (now Leningrad), and elsewhere to manage local affairs. Both the Provisional Government and the soviets felt, with reluctance, that the war against Germany should continue to be fought and that, in the new revolutionary situation, Russian troops would probably do better than heretofore. But they had bargained without the Bolsheviks the radical wing of the Russian revolutionary movement, whose leader, Lenin, had returned from his exile in Switzerland to Petrograd, with the tacit help of the Germans, in April. Lenin persuaded his followers to oppose the Provisional Government and all who wanted to continue fighting the war and emphasized the prior importance of a truly radical and international revolution of workers, peasants and intellectuals against the ruling classes of all countries.

By mid-summer, Petrograd was in a state of ferment. Lenin had gone into hiding again, but not before a series of armed street demonstrations had caused Kerensky to fear that his government was on the verge of being displaced by a Bolshevik revolution. At this point, the new Supreme Commander of the army, General Kornilov, started to lead troops—at Kerensky's request—to the capital in order to forestall any trouble that might break out. Kerensky then began to doubt the wisdom of his request; perhaps Kornilov, at the head of his troops, might try to oust the Provisional Government himself. At any event, Kerensky ordered Kornilov's advance to be stopped and the General himself to be arrested, and he also caused the Bolsheviks to be armed in a vain attempt to ingratiate himself with them against Kornilov and the army.

Kerensky's decision brought about the worst of all possible worlds from his point of view. The arming of the Bolsheviks helped to equip them for their eventual takeover in October. (Kornilov escaped from captivity and was eventually killed when fighting against the Bolsheviks in the civil war; and Kerensky died a 90-year-old exile in America in 1971.) But suppose Kerensky had not gone back on his decision to invite Kornilov and his troops to Petrograd but had decided, instead, to make a virtue out of what was, admittedly, a tricky situation . . .

2

It is August 1917. My government has just given the Bolsheviks

a bad fright by publishing a collection of documents which
confirm our worst suspicions that Lenin has been getting large
sums of money from the Germans to finance his defeatist
propaganda and fraternization campaign at the front. This
stab in the back was the cause of our defeat in Galicia! Lenin
has gone into hiding in fear of his life, and in Petrograd the
Bolsheviks have been turned against by the workers and
soldiers, who are enraged at having been manipulated to serve
the Germans. The Bolshevik Red Guards, as they call their
armed street-gangs, have been disarmed, their press has been
dismantled, many of their leaders are gaoled, and the Bolsheviks
at this moment are very much in retreat, lying low. I know that
now is the time to strengthen the morale and above all the
discipline of the army. The troops in the capital are afraid,
understandably, of being sent to our decomposing front, and at
the front itself the exhausted troops are being demoralized by
Leninist agitation to fraternize with the Germans across the
wire.

How much longer can I stand the strain? My nerves are getting worse all the time. I seem to be the only man who understands all the dangers in the situation. My new supreme
commander, Kornilov, is luckily the son of a poor Cossack and
an ardent defender of the Revolution, as he thinks he understands it, and thank God he is immensely popular. At his
urging, I restored the death penalty for cowardice, desertion
and looting at the front, and for seditious agitation in the rear,
hoping to restore discipline in the army, though applying these
measures is not so straightforward ...

The situation is so fluid, everything is so chaotic, so many
forces are pulling in so many directions, that I am not even sure
what solid ground I have to stand on. What can I be sure of?
Well, I am pretty sure that, despite all their slogans and banners,
the soldiers wandering the streets, and the workers who have
been idle for months, are not committed to the Bolsheviks, and
nor are they especially loyal to the Soviet, nor for that matter to
any other identifiable body. They are adrift ... As a socialist
and life-long defender of the democratic rights of the people,

I can't of course say this to anyone, but I know, as every Russian knows, that the Russians are a disorganized lot, easily led by tough leadership. Look how they turned against their heroes, the Bolsheviks, once we showed them up to be German agents, once we showed them the government was prepared to apply force in order to carry out the law! The key to the Russian mind is that it loves authority and detests weakness. Who came to Nicholas's rescue when he abdicated? Not a soul, not a single general would move troops to defend the dynasty without first getting an order to do so, and who would give such an order!? Authority, orders, hierarchy, that's what Russians understand, and it's what we democrats fought so long to change, and made the Revolution just for that!

But now is not the time to get into a philosophical argument with myself. The situation calls for practical measures, not philosophy. True, that's how Lenin looks at things—get the job done and ask questions later. And Kornilov—he wants urgent practical measures, first-aid, stop the rot, turn the tide! Can I, a life-long socialist, betray my progressive ideals and adopt tsarist police measures? But would it be a betrayal? Surely, my first duty is to see that our revolutionary ideals are not swallowed up in a terrible Russian defeat by the Germans, or by the forces of anarchy and chaos which profit from our tolerance, and which make possible a Bolshevik attempt at power.

And now I have asked Kornilov to send a strong, loyal force to Petrograd in case the Germans attack or the Bolsheviks start something like last July. Also, we've got to show the mobs that hang around the Soviet that we're in charge and that there'll be trouble if they don't rejoin the colours and take some orders, for a change.

That devil Lvov[1] is a headache. Who can trust an ex-Procurator of the Holy Synod? He has never actually shown me a single written statement in Kornilov's own hand of Kornilov's intentions. He tells me Kornilov thinks it's time for a new government, a strong one with him as its head and me as Minister of Justice. I don't like that part of it. Kornilov hasn't

William Ewart Gladstone

Alexander Kerensky reviewing
troops at the front, 1917

i Tojo in 1946

(Radio Times Hulton Picture Library)

Konrad Adenauer in 1952

Salvador Allende *(Christian Belpaire, Camera*

Alexander Dubcek (left) with Dr Gustav Husak

(Camera

my ability to see all sides of all questions, which is what a
Prime Minister must have. But if we now need a military
dictatorship. . . . I can't see the Soviet liking it, or liking me for
going along with it, but that's not all they're going to have to
swallow. . . .

Perhaps as Minister of Justice I would be a reassurance to
them that a strong-arm government would still respect legalities?
Actually, it might well appeal to a lot of people. After all, I am
widely popular and so is Kornilov. I'm still a force to be
reckoned with on the Left, and even the liberals seem to be
putting their faith in him. Together we would be unstoppable,
at least at this moment, when the Bolsheviks have lost their
footing. But we must act fast, because deserters and other riff-
raff are joining their ranks all the time. That just proves they're
afraid of what we might do to them as deserters. . . . Kornilov
seemed perfectly all right on the line just now, no threats or
anything, despite the fact that nothing was actually spelt out. . . .
Actually, in the end it was sensible of him to move Krymov
and his Savage Division[2] close to the city. I was worried about
them being too much of a provocation, but now the die is cast
the sooner they get here the better. Kornilov must come
himself. We'll show ourselves to the masses together, me, the
voice of the Revolution, the man they call the Persuader-in-
Chief—I quite like that—the only man who can weld the discipline of restraint onto the forces of democracy—with Kornilov's help. I must repress my distaste for such theatricals, and
for the sake of Russia, Kornilov and I must stand shoulder to
shoulder, literally. We'll find a grand balcony in the city—the
Kseshinskaya Palace! How Lenin will squirm when he hears
that Kerensky and Kornilov have stood together on the balcony
from which he used to inflame the mobs with his anarchist
bombast! Yes, we'll announce it in advance, and in front of us
we'll have lined up the Savage Division and all the loyal troops
to be found in the capital. It will be a military display of force
and determination.

And then I'll speak to them. I can tell them the Germans
are on their way and that we're all in danger. I'll tell them now is

not the time to argue about war aims or foreign policy. We can forget about all that. This is a revolutionary government and its first responsibility is to defend the Revolution in its moment of crisis: salus revolutionis lex prima est! Who said that? Never mind. Fellow Russians, don't you want to defend the Revolution and Mother Russia? The Leninists are lying when they tell you this is tsarist policy. To defend Revolutionary Russia is the duty and the right of every Russian democrat. And if we don't, then Lenin's allies, the Germans, will be here and will put an end to our revolution in quick time. My brothers, I know your sufferings. Why else do I bear the heavy burden of my responsibilities, if not to organize a just society that will ease those sufferings? But now is not the time to care for ourselves, only for Russia and the Revolution. To our long-suffering, humble peasant-brethren I say, the land is yours! We are holding it in trust for you and we will share it out justly among you when the enemy has been—er—stopped. . . .

I've never actually said that to them before. I think that with Kornilov alongside and the threat of disciplined troops right there, there is a good chance they may rally to us again. I'll tell them that Kornilov, a son of the people, is going to put backbone into the army again and that he is going to crush the enemy within, the German Bolshevik agents, the provocateurs, who call themselves soviet democrats, but who came back to Russian thanks only to their German paymasters, as everybody knows. I wonder how many Bolshevik sympathizers will go on calling themselves Bolsheviks or Leninists after they've heard that! They're all cowards. They'll come to heel when Kornilov cracks the whip! And once we've re-established order in the streets and put a curb on the army committees, our job will be to hold the Germans until the Americans get going on the western front. And even if we lose against the Germans, by not sueing for a separate peace we can expect to come out of the war reasonably intact, assuming the Allies beat the Germans in the end. And a victory for us would secure the democratic regime forever.

Yes, all things considered, this seems to be the right way to do it. Of course, that swine Lvov could be tricking me, lying to get me into a trap. . . . Kornilov could be planning a blood-bath, with me as his first victim. . . . I know a lot of those who are backing him hate me and everything I stand for. They'd like me out of the way. And the Soviet would not be sorry to see me go. . . . But the people! They wouldn't stand for it, surely? But by the time they knew of it, it would be too late. . . . I must put these ideas out of my head, I mustn't falter now. Kornilov's men are on their way and this may be the last chance we have, the last chance that I have of turning the tide of anarchy and of averting another rising by the Bolsheviks. . . .

3

Kerensky offers a fruitful subject for speculation precisely because he was a complex figure. His moods would swing from mania to depression quite as hectically as Lenin's did from euphoria to dejection. The extraordinary burden of responsi-bility that he quite inappropriately took on himself in the summer of 1917 had a number of effects on him. His well-developed powers of rhetoric and advocacy, tested to good effect in the law courts of the old regime, where he earned the reputa-tion of a fighter for the people's rights, now took flight, carrying him to literally dizzying heights. The nervous exhaustion these transports cost him was repaid with interest by the sense that he was commanding the very cross-roads of history: his last book is called *Russia and History's Turning-Point*, but was published in England accurately retitled *The Kerensky Memoirs*. His speeches in 1917, though not only his, are peppered with apocalypsis. On the negative side, the pressures on him drove him in on himself, generating highly emotional states, suspicion, fear of plots (some of which certainly existed), hysteria and confusion, unpredictability, all of which destroyed the confi-dence of those around him.

Not only was Kerensky, therefore, an ideal subject for the game of 'What if?' but so was the incident around which our invention has revolved, the 'Kornilov affair'. The essence of that incident is that, because Kerensky and Kornilov spoke to each other through unstable intermediaries, Kerensky was not absolutely sure that he understood Kornilov's intentions, and Kornilov was never sure whether Kerensky meant what he said from one minute to the next. Yet both were for a brief moment set on a common course, that of reasserting the authority of the government by means of a show of disciplined military force in the capital, and it is on this brief moment that our speculation has concentrated.

History tells us that the moment when Kerensky and Kornilov shared a common purpose was, in fact, very brief. The real Kerensky, as opposed to my invented one, quickly countermanded his order that Kornilov bring his troops to Petrograd. Why? Kerensky was suspicious that Kornilov's backers, and indeed the general himself, wanted him out of the way. Politically, Kerensky had become dangerously isolated, which only added to his growing distrust of almost everybody. As Prime Minister, his commitment to the army chiefs naturally laid him bare to his enemies on the Left, and his refusal to take decisive action against the disorder and lawlessness made him an object of contempt to the military leadership and the officer corps, who blamed him for army demoralization. Without doubt, too much was put on him and too much was expected of him, and making himself the linch-pin of an impossible combination pulled his mind and his will in different directions. It is the struggle of these polarized aims in his conflicted mind that make our fantasy plausible, the belief in his continued popular appeal and the dream of omnipotence through an ostentatious alliance with Kornilov. It is a Walter Mitty scene, perhaps, but one to which Kerensky, owing to the extraordinary stress of his position, might have been prone.

However confused Kerensky may have been at that time, at least one view we have imputed to him he shared with many others in Russia, then and since, and that is that the Russian mobs would obey harsh authority. The poet Zinaida Gippius wrote devastatingly of this on 9 November (27 October Old Style), 1917, in a poem called *Joy:* 'The vomit of the war, this wild joy of October/.../O poor and sinful, pitiable land of mine./.../Your people in their madness murdered their own freedom,/.../And soon a stick will drive you back into your stye,/You, nation, who respect not sacred things.'

It is of course impossible to say how Kornilov's troops would have acted or been greeted in the capital in reality, for the plan was aborted in mid-flight. But it is probable that he would have been welcomed as the conquering hero by cheering crowds of soldiers and workers, so long as they had been assured he was coming to 'defend the revolution'.

From Kerensky's point of view, Kornilov was undoubtedly a mixed blessing, for although he was a 'son of the people', those who backed him were to become the spearhead leaders of the civil war to come, enemies of the soviets and advocates, not of monarchy, but of authoritarian rule, anti-democratic. Given that these facts were fairly general knowledge in the capital, where rumours of an impending military putsch were rife—along with every other kind of rumour—the main flaw in our imaginary reconstruction of events is to suppose that the arming of the Bolsheviks and the pro-government agitation of Kornilov's troops, depended solely on Kerensky's authority, whereas in fact the news of Kornilov's advance had a self-electrifying effect on the soviets, and the rearming of the Bolsheviks may have taken place regardless of Kerensky's intentions, though it was his panic that mobilized the Soviet.

Even so, the armed detachments that did go out to 'defend the revolution' against Kornilov, did not engage in armed combat, but only propaganda warfare, urging the opposition not to fight their brothers in the capital: it seems that even Caucasian Muslims were as susceptible as their Russian comrades-in-arms to this kind of solidarist agitation. With that in mind, however, it remains possible that, had they arrived in Petrograd as expected, Kornilov's forces would not have encountered armed resistance. In that event, the plan might have gone ahead, leading Bolsheviks might have been publicly shot for treason, and a measure of White Terror exercised against leading soviet elements, in which case the fantasized sequence of later events is not wholly implausible. The American entry into the war did not weigh until about the time of the Bolshevik seizure of power, which suggests that a success by Kornilov and Kerensky in September would have meant the Germans' keeping their strength up on the Eastern Front for longer than they in fact did, and even if the Russians had in the end lost, it is not likely that a government dominated by ex-tsarist generals would have bargained away Russia's western borderlands as readily as Lenin did. In the still likely event of a Russian civil war, Allied intervention on the side of a pro-war government, in command of central administration and the reins of power, rather than the scattered and peripheral, disunited forces of the White armies as they were, would perhaps have prevented the establishment of a socialist regime indefinitely. . . .

The gamble in our imagined act by Kerensky would consist in the belief that the soviets at that time were not prepared to challenge the government for full power, and indeed it was only the Bolsheviks, once they had been rearmed through Kerensky's and the soviet's panic, and had achieved majorities in the Petrograd and Moscow Soviets in early November, who were prepared to take power. As for whether Kerensky could have decided to act as we have imagined, the fact that he belonged to a party that condoned terrorism, that he himself had advocated removal of the Tsar by assassination, if necessary, and that he encouraged Kornilov to think he was in favour of harsh measures, is proof enough that his democratic convictions may not have been so deeply rooted, and that the soul of Russian pragmatism struggled with that of constitutional restraint within his breast.

It is also possible that the Kerensky of our imagination was right and that Kornilov, had he and his terrible cohort reached the capital, would have created a general bloodbath and dropped Kerensky into the middle of it. That Alexander Fedorovich Kerensky extricated himself alive from the chaos and the danger of his personal position in November, that he managed to outlive all his rivals and, in the peaceful and ordered surroundings of Stanford and Oxford, look back at those stormy times from a distance of fifty years, suggests that his instinct for survival was highly developed. Perhaps, looking at it from his point of view, the decision he took, not to trust Kornilov, was after all the rational one?

NOTES

1 V. N. Lvov was the chief go-between for Kerensky and Kornilov, and was largely responsible for their mutual misunderstandings. Lvov purported to convey plans back and forth, but showed written material to neither of his principals. He played some deep and provocative game of his own for unknown sinister reasons. Kerensky had him arrested at the time of his change of mind over Kornilov. He ended up working for the Soviet regime.

2 When Kerensky first asked Kornilov to send a strong force to Petrograd, he requested that they should not include the 'Savage' Division of Caucasian Muslim troops, nor General Krymov. He suspected Krymov as a conspirator, and he feared that the arrival of the Savage Division would be too obvious a counter-revolutionary move.

If I had been . . .

HIDEKI TOJO IN 1941

'How I would have avoided bombing Pearl Harbor.'

LOUIS ALLEN

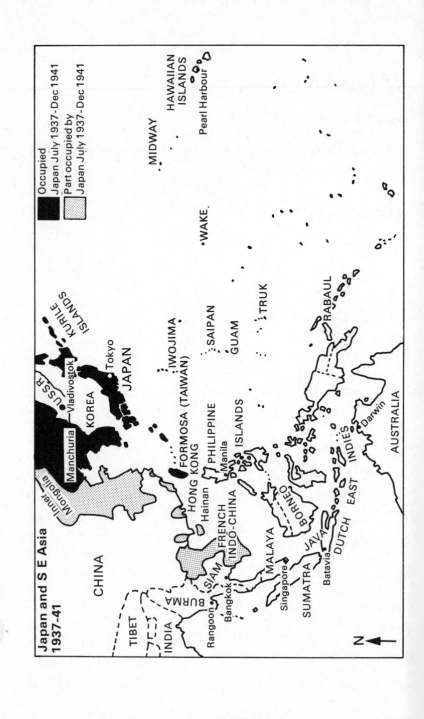

Japan and S E Asia 1937-41

■ Occupied
Japan July 1937 - Dec 1941

▦ Part occupied by
Japan July 1937 - Dec 1941

CHINA

TIBET

INDIA

BURMA

Rangoon

Bangkok

SIAM

FRENCH
INDO-CHINA

Inner
Mongolia

Manchuria

USSR

Vladivostok

KOREA

Tokyo

JAPAN

KURILE
ISLANDS

Hainan

HONG KONG

FORMOSA (TAIWAN)

IWOJIMA

Manila

PHILIPPINE
ISLANDS

SAIPAN

GUAM

Singapore

MALAYA

SUMATRA

Batavia

JAVA

BORNEO

DUTCH EAST
INDIES

Darwin

AUSTRALIA

TRUK

RABAUL

WAKE

MIDWAY

HAWAIIAN
ISLANDS

Pearl Harbour

N

1

Lieutenant-General Hideki Tojo became Prime Minister of Japan on October 17, 1941. He had previously been War Minister, and continued to hold that portfolio as well as that for home affairs, which he held until February 1942. Born in 1884, he came of a military family, his father having been a major-general in the Russo-Japanese war. Tojo's first big appointment was in 1935, as commander of the military police (Kempei) of the Kwantung Army in Manchuria. He later became Chief of Staff of that army, then Vice-Minister for War in 1938, and War Minister in Prince Konoye's 1940 cabinet.

When he was appointed Prime Minister, the Emperor gave him to understand that he was not bound by the decision of the September 6, 1941 Imperial Conference between the Japanese Cabinet and the Supreme Command which laid down Japan's policy on peace and war: namely, that if Japan could not obtain satisfaction of her demands by early October, a decision should be taken to open war on the USA, Great Britain, and the Netherlands. So Tojo had carte blanche. At first he strove for a diplomatic solution, but he decided not to make any concession to the American demand that Japan withdraw troops from China before the USA would lift the economic embargo on Japan, imposed in June 1941, and this refusal invited similar American intransigence. The American Secretary of State, Cordell Hull, addressed a note to the Japanese, which reached them on November 28, 1941, in which Japan was offered a new deal provided she withdrew all troops from China and French Indo-China, ceased to support her puppet regime in China, broke her alliance with Germany, and signed a non-aggression pact with the USA, Britain, Holland, China, Russia and Thailand. The Japanese Cabinet found the Note's conditions unacceptable. Two further conferences were held to stave off war, but the irrevocable decision was finally made on December 1, 1941. In readiness, the Japanese fleet had already left its anchorage in the Kuriles on November 26, and struck the American fleet anchored at Pearl Harbor on December 7.

The war was a series of brilliant rapid victories for Japan, followed by the slow stalemate of 1943 and 1944. By the summer of 1944 the Americans had a forward base on Saipan, well within Japan's 'inner defence perimeter'. On June 18, 1944, Tojo resigned as Prime Minister, an office he had held for two years and nine months of the most crucial period in Japan's modern history. When the war ended, over a year later, and Japan was occupied, an American unit was sent to arrest him. To an American journalist who had called on him before his arrest, Tojo had already made his stand clear. He knew he would be tried as a war criminal, but he intended to remove any suggestion that the Emperor was involved in responsibility for the war: 'I was responsible for the war. I accept full and complete responsibility. But I do not believe that makes me a war criminal. There is a difference between leading a nation in a war which it believes right and just, and being a war criminal. . . . But the victor decides that.'

When the American unit arrived, Tojo attempted to commit suicide by shooting himself. The attempt failed, and he became the prime target of the International Military Tribunal for the Far East, which sat in Tokyo from May 1946 to November 1948. Joseph B. Keenan, an American expert on criminal law and formerly head of the Criminal Division of the Department of Justice, was the chief prosecutor. In spite of the misty haze of a language barrier between Tojo and himself, his own frequent inebriation, and feuding with the court president, the Australian judge Sir William Webb, Keenan obtained the conviction of Tojo on charges of criminal conspiracy to wage aggressive war, and ultimate responsibility for the many atrocities committed by the

*Japanese armies in the field and occupied territories. Tojo was
found guilty on November 12, 1948. He composed a poem on
the morning sentence was passed:*

> I look up and hear
> A voice from on high
> The Buddha calling, clear,
> From the pure and infinite sky.

*The Buddhist chaplain, Dr Hanayama, saw Tojo several times
in prison. On the eve of their execution, Dr Hanayama read aloud
a sacred Buddhist text to Tojo and his three colleagues who were
to die that day—Doihara, Matsui, and Muto. Then all four
shouted* Banzai! *six times, three for the Emperor, three for
Japan. They walked to the death block murmuring the invocation*
Namu Amida Butsu (*We pray to the compassionate Buddha*).

*At one and a half minutes past midnight, December 23, 1948,
Tojo was hanged in Sugamo Prison.*

*I imagine him there, still as a war criminal, but as the result
of a different war, the night before his execution, thinking about
what he actually did, and what he might have done.*

2

Meditation in Sugamo, December 22, 1948

There can be few things less profitable than a defeated general
mulling over his defeats, re-fighting his battles so that this time
he wins them, in his head. And yet, it's not more difficult for
me to do this than to accept, as I must, the moral responsibility
for bringing my people into war and my Emperor into the hands
of his enemies. Of course no one who knows our Japanese
system of government will believe that I alone was responsible.
That is the foreign picture of me as a dictator like Hitler, and

our government, even in wartime, was never so totalitarian. But my role was great. I cannot—would not—deny that. On the other hand, anyone else, with my background and training, would have fulfilled the same role and brought his country at any rate to the edge of war. The ways of the Buddha are unfathomable.

It all started because we were being strangled by those in comfortable possession of the riches of the earth. They made laws which ensured they held what they had. Were we supposed to respect those laws, and starve in penury, with our industries running to a standstill? The Americans could not see that for us to make war on China was like rebuking an unruly member of the same family: it was an internal conflict in Asia. We were the only Asians who had stood on our own feet and fought back when the Europeans and Americans laid hands on us in the nineteenth century. We respected China. Was she not the cradle of our civilization? We wanted her to shrug off her decadence and stand up for herself. I wanted this for India, too.

Not for Manchuria, no. But then Manchuria was a special case, not part of China anyway. The sea between us didn't prevent Manchuria being *our* hinterland. I think this is what misled me in the 1930s. My time in Manchuria made me fear the endless threat of Russia, like a ring round our borders. Passion is a bad strategist. My anger with America—Japan's anger with America—should not have blinded me. It misled me into allowing preparations for war against America to go ahead.

The real conflict was not with the USA. We needed to keep the US Pacific Fleet at all costs from interfering with our expeditions to the Southern Regions. That was where our national interests lay. Of course, we'd had the US as a hypothetical enemy for many years. Every General Staff makes plans and exercises against a potential enemy without actually going to war, or even intending to. What profit was there for us in turning the world's biggest industrial giant into our enemy? And doing likewise with Soviet Russia? Ideology and the defence of Manchuria might turn us against the Russians but we did not, in 1941, have the sinews to sustain a long campaign against them. So we had to turn south and look for those sinews. What we had to have is what every industrial nation has to have: oil. There was oil for the taking in the Netherlands East Indies. Once the Dutch were defeated in 1940—I was Vice-Minister for War then—we tried every kind of pressure short of war to make them supply what we needed. They refused. All the tricks and heavy persuasion that had worked with the French in Indo-China failed to move the Dutch. Our course then was quite clear.

The Netherlands East Indies—Java, Sumatra, Borneo—became our real target. A successful strategy would have been based on interest, not on passion, and would have reduced risks, not increased them. It would have isolated the Dutch in Java —and Great Britain which supported the Dutch—and then used force or the threat of force. After all, we took over French Indo-China in two stages, and the first stage was complete in the summer of 1940. Why could we not make the same process work with the Netherlands East Indies?

One reason was that the United States slapped their economic embargo on us. But that embargo took place a whole year after we decided to put pressure on South-East Asia. By the autumn of 1941, Russia was occupied with the German invasion; Great Britain had undergone defeat after defeat (Norway, the Low Countries, France, Yugoslavia, Greece, Crete); France and Holland were under German occupation. Only the US was out of the war. So our aim should have been to obtain the oil resources of the Netherlands East Indies without incurring military reprisals from Britain or the US.

The British I was sure of. They were working closely with the Dutch in the Netherlands East Indies, and putting pressure on the Thais to resist our gradual and inexorable infiltration into Thailand. But we knew that they—or some of them—had put out peace feelers to the Germans in 1940, and the 'Appreciation of the Situation in the Far East' of their Chiefs of Staff was in our hands a short time after it was drafted. We owed this to a British Air Chief Marshal's supposition that the sea-route was safer than the air-route for highly secret documents, and to the shrewdness of a German submarine commander who torpedoed a Blue Funnel ship in the Indian Ocean and had the wit to search it for documents before sending it to the bottom. So I knew the British would be on the defensive as far as we were concerned throughout 1941. They did not want to go to war with us, and we could flex our muscles against them, to an almost extreme degree, and still be sure they would not react to anything other than a direct invasion of their overseas territories.

Two strategies were possible: an attack on the Netherlands East Indies, which would include an attack on Malaya and Borneo, but keeping the US neutral; or an attack on the Netherlands East Indies hoping to keep *both* Great Britain and the US neutral.

Would they intervene if we went straight for Java? I wondered about this. Both of them must have considered that Java involved their own interests directly and our getting oil from Java and Sumatra would have nullified the American economic embargo at once. And yet . . . Neither the British nor the Americans had done anything to help the French in Indo-China in July 1940, any more than the US had intervened to save Paul Reynaud and his government from the Germans the month before. So it was sensible to leave the Philippines and Hawaii strictly alone, and keep American opinion still divided. Did not Byrnes, then a Supreme Court Justice and later Secretary of State, say that if Roosevelt had asked Congress to declare war on Japan in November 1941 he would have been defeated by a two-thirds majority?

At that time, a lot of my cabinet colleagues were arguing in favour of our making overt war on the USA and it was Kido who managed to bring that dangerous talk to an end. Temporarily, at least. On October 12, 1941, we all met at the home of the Prime Minister, Prince Konoye, to hear what Kido had to say. The Marquis Kido was His Majesty's closest confidential adviser, and his go-between in important matters of state. So there was an inkling where his views came from, and they demanded respect. And, too, it was Konoye's birthday. I was not in a birthday mood. The nub of the matter, from the Americans' point of view, was the fact that Japan maintained troops in China. Naturally enough, since I'd fought in China, there was no prospect I would less rather face than withdrawing our troops; but I did wonder about the possible advantages of a diplomatic gesture. I knew the Navy wanted to continue to negotiate with the Americans, yet they would not come out openly and say so. I was determined to force the Navy's hand, so I said bluntly, 'There's no point in pursuing talks with Washington.' Oikawa, the Navy Minister, was forced into the open, and had to say he thought we must give up preparations for war and continue with negotiations for peace; and that he left the decision to the Prime Minister.

Konoye knew there were risks whichever way we opted, but said he wanted to go on negotiating. I wasn't sure the diplomats of the Foreign Ministry themselves believed in the upshot of negotiations, so I turned to Admiral Toyoda, the Foreign Minister, and asked him if *he* had any confidence in them. He didn't answer, but Konoye answered for him: 'I still choose to negotiate.'

'You can't prevail on the Army General Staff,' I answered. 'I want to hear what Toyoda thinks.' As I expected he would, Toyoda answered that there was no point in continuing talks if the Army wouldn't budge over the presence of our troops in China. Wasn't some compromise possible?

The stationing of troops in China was a matter of life and death for the Army, I replied. No concessions on that score.

I knew the Army would back me in this. What I did not fully realize at the time was the justice of Konoye's answer: that it was possible to agree with America *formally*, agree to withdraw all troops in principle, and then negotiate an agreement with the Chinese to leave troops in certain areas. I didn't think Konoye understood the Chinese mentality. Once we agreed to withdraw, they would take it as a sign of weakness. It would not move them towards compromise, but stiffen their will to resist.

Besides which, was it possible to make a pledge to America with the intention of secretly dishonouring it? Konoye didn't seem to mind doing this. I couldn't stomach it. I was wrong.

What stuck in my throat, I'm afraid, was that Konoye was trying to reverse the decision of the Imperial Conference of September 6, 1941. We'd decided then that if the negotiations with the US showed no signs of coming to a successful conclusion by October 10, we should move towards a decision for war. That decision was to be reached jointly by the supreme command and the government, not, as Oikawa seemed (sycophantically or irresponsibly) to imply, by the Prime Minister, Konoye himself. I said this. I also said I didn't think we'd get a diplomatic solution, to which Konoye replied sarcastically that he would prefer to leave war to a person confident of victory.

This seemed slippery to me. Hadn't we *already* decided to go to war if diplomacy failed? When Konoye said that this was really a decision among ourselves and could be reconsidered, with the Emperor's approval, it seemed to me he was speaking of an Imperial decision as if it were unofficial. I could hardly contain myself. But Suzuki intervened. He had on his mind the young officers' rebellion of 1936, and asked how he could control the army if preparations for war were abandoned. That didn't worry me so much. I would bring recalcitrants to heel if that became necessary. By the end of the afternoon, it was clear they had accepted my view that troops must be stationed in China, as a barrier to the spread of communism into Korea and Manchuria. On the other hand, negotiations would go on until October 15. But, on the way back to Tokyo, the Navy's shillyshallying worried me. How could we go to war if they were so weak in their support?

The head of the Military Affairs Section of Imperial General Headquarters, Colonel Sato, offered me a way out, and like a pig-headed idiot I turned it down. 'I'll fix up a meeting in private for you,' he offered, 'with the two Chiefs of Staff and the Navy Minister. Not at the Ministry, but at a geisha house. You can then probe the Navy's lack of confidence, and offer to

take on yourself the responsibility of not fighting. It won't
be easy. But it would remove their diffidence about coming
out into the open and saying they don't want war.' Sato was
right. An informal geisha-house chat would have done the trick.
Instead, I got on my high horse and asked him if he really
thought the Navy Minister would say in a geisha house what he
refused to say at an Imperial Conference. An opportunity lost:
a geisha party was exactly where Oikawa would have opened
up.

Anyway, Konoye tried to put pressure on me again. Before
the 10 a.m. cabinet meeting of October 14, 1941, he phoned
and suggested we should promise 'the formality' of withdrawal
from China. My reaction was that the US would behave as I
suggested the Chinese would. They'd take it as a sign we were
weakening under pressure, and this would be a signal for more
pressure, not less. I must admit I despised Konoye at that
moment. He was a weak specimen, I thought. I told him we
should sometimes in our lives be ready to jump off the veranda
of the Kiyomizu Temple—a leap into the unknown—and he
answered that that was all very well for an individual, but not
for someone in a responsible position. I couldn't help pointing
out, scornfully, that the basic issue between us was clearly a
difference of personality. . . .

In the cabinet meeting the Foreign Minister, Toyoda,
declared that the US was more and more suspicious of Japan's
attitude, talking peace and preparing for war at the same time.
I argued that to make a concession about withdrawal from
China would be defeat at the hands of the US. If we withdrew
from China, we would lose Manchuria and Korea. I lost my
temper with Oikawa because he refused to say openly whether
the Navy thought they could beat the Americans or not.

Konoye and the rest of them simply sat under this outburst,
cowed. I don't mean by me, but by the force—the Japanese
Army—they knew I spoke for. The upshot was that the President of the Cabinet Planning Board, a few hours later, called
on me to say that Konoye wouldn't go on. If I insisted on
maintaining my position, he would resign. His resignation

would solve nothing, in my view: whether Konoye stayed or went, the Navy still hadn't pronounced itself. I suggested to Suzuki that only a member of the Imperial Family would bring a conclusion out of the impasse, and that Prince Higashikuni should be brought in to take over the premiership from Konoye. If we were to be refused a decision for war, then it might have to be the weight of an Imperial prince's decision which would ensure there was no revolt among the army officers. No question of His Majesty doing this himself. It would be unconstitutional, and he had a high regard for the Meiji Constitution, as indeed he had for anything to do with his grandfather the Emperor Meiji.

Kido was not enthusiastic for Higashikuni. I could see why. The prince was a general, with little experience of politics. If war came, it would directly involve the Imperial family if Higashikuni were the head of a cabinet which brought it about. The Imperial family might in turn become the object of hatred on the part of the Japanese people. An unthinkable situation. At least, unthinkable then.

I think Kido would have preferred Oikawa to succeed Konoye, since the third Konoye cabinet had fallen because of my opposition, and to appoint me would look like a surrender to the Army's intransigent demands. On the other hand, the Navy was dragging its heels, whereas the Army constituted a problem of potential rebelliousness. That was where the strength lay. There was a risk that naming me would make the US think that Japan was definitely bound on a course for war. On the other hand, if I were Premier, they would be convinced that if a decision for peace *were* reached, then it would bind the army. Konoye agreed with this case, and added, when Kido consulted him about a possible successor, that the Emperor should order me to dispense with the September 6 decision and start afresh.

All this I heard afterwards, because when the *jūshin*[1] were conferring about the succession, I was at the War Ministry packing my papers. Late in the afternoon of October 17, I was told His Majesty wished to see me immediately. 'We direct you to form a cabinet,' he told me, 'and to abide by the provisions of the

Constitution. We believe that an exceedingly grave situation confronts the nation. Bear in mind, at this time, that cooperation between the army and navy should be closer than ever before. It is Our intention to summon the Navy Minister also and to speak to him in the same vein.'

I was too surprised to accept at once, and asked for a few moments to consider. After His Majesty spoke to Oikawa, the Navy Minister joined me in the waiting-room. Kido came in. In addition to cooperation between the Army and Navy, Kido said, His Majesty wished the situation at home and abroad to be studied afresh without any bounds being imposed by the Imperial Conference decision of September 6. I had emphasized in cabinet that the decisions of that conference, being made in His Majesty's presence, could not lightly be set aside. Yet here he was, in effect, setting them aside for us himself. If I accepted the premiership, it was clearly a case of *hakushi kangen*—carte blanche.

I went at once to the Meiji Shrine and then to the Yasukuni Shrine to pay homage. Then I returned to the War Ministry. I hope I gave General Muto the right impression when I brushed aside his sheet of paper giving a list of proposed cabinet appointments. They were not going to meddle with *me*.

I was now Prime Minister and was free to revise the decision on the date for going to war. The revision needed speed. As Admiral Nagano pointed out during a liaison conference between cabinet and supreme command, the Navy—in peacetime—was using up four hundred tons of oil an hour. We needed oil. And we needed to try to avoid war. . . .

(My time must be very near now. I have asked for the priest Hanayama to be with me at the end. He will give Katsuko the poems I have written for her. I know I shall return to my country as a Buddha, just as my body will be re-absorbed into the soil of Japan. I am ready to hear the summons. In fact, I have already heard it. When I was out in the exercise yard a few days ago, I heard someone playing the bamboo flute, the *shakuhachi.* I wrote a *tanka* about it:

> *The notes of the shakuhachi*
> *Trill like the notes of the roller-bird*
> *But in my ears it sounds*
> *Like the summons of Amida Buddha.*

Yes, it is very near, now.)

. . . I didn't intervene much in the liaison conferences after assuming the premiership. I wanted every minister to speak his mind, and hear what he had to say. Three plans emerged. One, to stick it out and not to declare war even if diplomacy with the US came to nothing. Two, to declare war at once (the supreme command wanted this, but it was clearly contrary to the Emperor's wish that we should think the whole thing afresh). Three, to go ahead with diplomatic efforts while completing preparations to go to war if they failed. Three was an obvious compromise, which put the decision for war a little later than the September 6 conference had done. Finally, on November 1, 1941, everyone lost his temper on the fixing of a terminal date for diplomatic negotiations to succeed. The Navy thought November 30, the Army November 13. The Navy's view prevailed, and then I asked if it would be possible to add a 24-hour postponement, making it December 1. The Vice-Chief of the Naval General Staff, Tsukada, promptly said it was out of the question, but Shimada, Oikawa's successor as Navy Minister, smoothed things over by saying we could use midnight November 30 as a compromise.

I told the Imperial Conference on November 5, 1941, that I thought prospects for reaching a friendly settlement by negotiation were dim, but that our proposals did represent an attempt to go some way towards meeting American demands. The Chief of the Naval General Staff assured us that, if it came to war and there was a mid-ocean battle between the two fleets, our Navy was ready. . . .

(This sounds like the priest Hanayama coming now. Namu Amida Butsu. Namu Amida Butsu. Namu Amida Butsu.)

... The important thing for us to do was to drive a wedge between the Americans and the British. The handling of such a split required finesse—but I had, after all, when I was a young officer, been known as 'kamisori' or 'the razor-sharp mind'. There had been moments of profound mistrust between the British and the Americans, as we knew. Yardley's[2] revelation to us that he had been breaking diplomatic ciphers on America's behalf very naturally led us to think that if the USA had evolved a cipher-breaking technique, then the British most certainly had done the same. They had. And one of the first things they did with it, apart from cracking the codes of the Bolsheviks, was to investigate the poison gas strength of the United States. Not the action of a potential ally. And it was an American who made the case, less than a decade before the outbreak of war between Britain and Germany, that the USA and Britain were already at war economically, at any rate in certain major areas of their economy. Ludwell Denny's *America Conquers Britain* was written in 1930, and describes an economic war for copper, nickel, rubber, oil, nitrates, aircraft, shipping, and cables. Denny exploded what he called 'the dear cousin myth', the myth that a common language, literature, law and political tradition made war unthinkable. 'This is,' he wrote, 'another of those pretty notions about the nature of war which violate experience. Historically, blood and language kinship has meant war more often than peace. ... And the civil wars of Britain and America have been especially unreasoning, vindictive and bloody. If brother fought brother in our War of the States, by what costly forgetfulness can anyone assume that cousin will refuse to fight cousin because of kinship?' He was not speaking of the German-American Bund, which was simply a channel of Nazi propaganda into the USA, but of the deeper, more essential conflict which, in his view, set a fading Empire, becoming poorer day by day, in opposition to a rich and energetic younger power, with ambition and the industrial drive to back it.

In the winter of 1940, when it seemed quite feasible that Germany would knock Great Britain out of the war, our Army Operations Section had a paper drawn up by a young staff officer, Captain Sejima, on the possibility of driving a wedge between Britain and the USA. I remember he made a very interesting case. 'Japan's chief aim,' he pointed out, 'is to secure raw material from the Dutch East Indies. Britain and Holland are united in keeping us out. But there is no need for us to fight the USA. A war against America, in terms of scale and duration, would be a terrifying thing to undertake. Such a war, in any case, flies in the face of our Army's national purpose.' 'How do you understand that?' was the natural question. 'It is to defend our patrimony,' he answered, 'and our patrimony is Manchuria, against possible incursions from the Soviet Union.' 'I can see,' I told him, 'that you are under no illusions about who is the real, permanent enemy in East Asia.' 'No, but we must draw the conclusions from that,' he answered. 'If we are to mount an operation into South-East Asia, then it is necessary at all costs to continue to be able to defend our homeland and Manchuria. The Army there should on no account be weakened. It follows that the burden of war, the operational scale, should not be complicated by drawing the USA into battle. We should only consider the invasion of South-East Asia if we are sure the US will keep out. This means investigating the possibility of separating the vital interests of the USA from those of Great Britain and Holland.

'There's no need to look for a dramatic wedge, separating the two powers on a massive, irreconcilable scale,' he went on. 'We should play on the notion of such a separation in the first phases of an operation in the south. Use diplomacy to demonstrate that the US interest is not vitally involved in assisting the retention of the old colonial empires. There are enough Americans ready to believe this as it is. They haven't lifted a finger to help the French in Indo-China. Let's see that they draw the logical conclusion from *that* piece of non-intervention.

'After we've acted successfully in the South, the results of the operation itself will radically improve our stance. So a long-term perspective is not vital.'

Unfortunately, Sejima was less than clear about *how* the object, the separation, was to be achieved. But there was an idea to build on, so I placed great stress on the success of negotiations between the USA and ourselves, which of course made the outcome depend on the concessions demanded from us by the USA. Even so, early in November 1941, I still thought there was a fifty-fifty chance of avoiding war with the USA.

Of course I prepared for war at the same time. But the proviso remained that if negotiations with the US were successful by midnight of December 1, the use of force would be suspended.

I offered what I thought was as far as we could go: if we could reach peace with China, we would withdraw troops from China, other than from Hainan Island, Inner Mongolia, and certain parts of North China. These would in their turn be evacuated, but later. I realized the Americans would want to know what 'later' meant, and our diplomats were instructed to say '25 years'. After such a peace, we would also withdraw troops from French Indo-China. And we would accept non-discriminatory trade in China if the principle were accepted on a world-wide basis. To quell US fears about joint action with Germany and Italy, our allies in the Tripartite Pact which we'd joined over a year before, the US was to be told that Japan would 'act independently'.

Another set of proposals was put forward, in which we suggested that the USA should cooperate in enabling us to have material from the Dutch East Indies, that they should restore trade relations to what they were before they froze our assets that summer; and that we should pull our troops in Southern French Indo-China back into the North of that country and ultimately, in the signing of peace with China, out of it alto-gether. After our efforts of the past decade to secure our position —over a million casualties in China—I do not see that we could have offered more.

That's what I put to the Conference on November 5, 1941.

It seems incredible, but the Navy had evolved a gambler's strategy of boldness, just as we were negotiating. It was, of course, Yamamoto's idea. Konoye had had him over to his private residence and sounded him out about what the Navy could do if, by some mischance, we were forced into war with America. Yamamoto had been to college there, and knew the place and the people. *'Ichinen-kan nara jūbun ni abarete mimashō. Sore kara saki wa dekimasen.'* A crisp reply, and a sound warning. 'If it's for a year, I can show them some strong-arm stuff. From then onwards, I can guarantee nothing.' The strong-arm included, it appeared, a naval air strike against the American base at Hawaii. He thought, and I agreed, that he could get away with it. But his reply to Konoye showed that he knew the end product of such a strike would be to bring the whole Pacific armoury of the US round our ears. A flamboyant gesture, yes, but it wouldn't have produced any long-term results at all. But the imaginative boldness of it struck me; and I thought, if we can envisage boldness of this kind which will *not* produce long-term results, why not a similar audacity in the diplomatic field, which will?

That is what I did. I made my offer to the United States which placed on *them* the onus of preserving the peace. Withdraw from China, they said. We will, I answered. Withdraw from French Indo-China, they said. We will, I answered. I left the time scale, and how and where, to detailed Foreign Ministry negotiations; but the acquiescence turned the heat off. At that point, the commercial pressure inside America to resume trading with us forced the blockade to break. Once we'd agreed to pull out of China, there was no reason to blackmail us any longer with the oil embargo.

I took a risk, then. We must not be vulnerable to such an embargo again, and that meant securing oil elsewhere. I gambled on the US and Great Britain hesitating to intervene if we mounted an expedition to the Dutch East Indies to force them to give us oil. We'd already made an initial move towards peace in China. And I knew we could make it known to powerful business interests in the USA that our views and theirs coincided

about the danger from the USSR. We'd already established a
channel to Frank Walker, Roosevelt's Postmaster General,
through the Catholic missionaries Drought and Walsh. I told
Iwakuro, who'd been in Washington with the two missionaries
before, to use them to emphasize our real strategic objective in
East Asia: the defence of the area from penetration by Russian
communism. I'd played skilfully on two American phobias
jointly: their fear of communism, and their unwillingness to
shed American blood to defend European colonial empires.
Roosevelt himself had no more intention than we had of allowing India, Burma, Malaya, Hong Kong and the rest to remain
for ever in British hands; and his views on the behaviour of
the French in Indo-China, I had it on reliable authority, would
have warmed the hearts of our General Staff.

The British were more difficult. Public opinion had been
roused against us for some time, and they had the Netherlands
government-in-exile in London. But in the end, I knew they
didn't want to risk going to war against us unless we attacked
them directly. So when we went into the Dutch East Indies,
the British did what they did when we first went into Indo-
China: nothing.

There was, inevitably perhaps, trouble here in Japan. The
kind of crisis we went through in 1936, when young officers
of the Army attempted a coup against the government, was
repeated, this time against me. Even Koga, my own son-in-law,
was involved! How he asked, could I be so craven and give in
to American pressure? But I had anticipated this, and I had no
intention of allowing young officer hotheads to wreck my plans.
A few propitiatory suicides by lax commanders, and secret
promises that the Army would be engaged sooner or later against
the Soviets, in Manchuria—the thing soon fizzled out.

But I meant those promises. And there was an instrument
ready to deliver the Russians into our hands. In spite of the first
strong German penetrations into Russia in the summer of 1941,
the USSR had maintained its Far Eastern forces in Siberia in
great strength. They were still edgy about the Kwantung Army,
and they'd given it a bloody nose at Nomonhan in 1939. So I

had to reduce their strength on the Manchurian border.

It was reported to me in October 1941 that the *Frankfurter Zeitung* correspondent in Tokyo, Richard Sorge, was in fact a Soviet spy. The revelation was astounding enough in itself, since he was a member of the Nazi Press Association, but there were Japanese involved, too, including Ozaki, who'd been a confidential adviser to Konoye. I wondered at first if the police had been on the wrong track, misled by the fact that Sorge was a drunk and a womanizer; but since his standing seemed pretty high with Ott, the German ambassador, I told them not to arrest him, but keep him under surveillance. They'd meant to bring him in for questioning, apparently, the very day I was made Premier, so it was fortunate I'd intervened.

Sorge, without knowing it, presented me with the perfect channel for the *yami jōhō* (black intelligence) I needed. If the Russians thought we were planning a move against them from Manchuria, they would keep more of their forces in the East. If, via Konoye and Ozaki, Sorge could feed into Red Army Intelligence false figures about the diminution of the Kwangtung Army and the alteration of our Order of Battle in Manchuria to suggest that our strength was being directed south, into the Pacific, they they would not hesitate to send more troops to the front in Europe. Which is precisely what happened. Our German allies, of course, bore the brunt of this intoxication, but they had not consulted us about their tergiversation in 1939, so I felt not a twinge of remorse on their behalf.

For our next move, it was necessary to keep Britain's attention focused elsewhere. Here, as with Sorge, the solution was ready to hand. Subhas Chandra Bose had escaped from British house arrest in India in 1941, and, via Afghanistan, Uzbekistan, and Moscow, had reached Germany. He was lucky to make it when he did. A few months' delay, and the German frontier would have turned into a battlefront. We got him back by submarine and infiltrated him into India in 1942. It was the best year. India was on the boil, and 'Quit India' signs were splashed over the walls of every Indian city. Within weeks, Bose set India ablaze.

Whatever we chose to do now, Britain's forces, such as they were, in the Far East, already had more than enough on their hands. The Russians were occupied with the Germans striking far into the Ukraine. The Americans had already, whatever Roosevelt wished, made us the necessary oil concessions and had failed to intervene when our fleet stood off Batavia. The time had come to make an even more direct appeal to the USA.

I launched the Kwantung Army out of Manchuria in the autumn of 1942. There was, of course, the risk of getting bogged down in winter operations, but my judgement proved right. The Russians, thanks to our Sorge deception (he was still blithely feeding radio intoxication to them, convinced of its accuracy because it came from Konoye), had reduced their strength in Siberia below the danger level. Vladivostok fell almost at once, Irkutsk within a month. It was the ideological adventure the Japanese Army had been waiting for. The generals who, as young men, remembered the Japanese intervention in Siberia in 1921, wanted to push as far west as the Urals, and join up with the German army which was still at the gates of Stalingrad. But I never envisaged Japan permanently occupying Russia up to the Urals, and ordered them to halt on the line of the Yenisei. Yamashita was in Krasnoyarsk when the order arrived not to advance further, and he was livid. He ascribed it, naturally enough, to personal motives, but it was nothing of the kind. I wanted another source of oil in Siberia, not endless steppe and desert. And, too, a wider buffer zone against a triumphant Germany seemed wise. After the fall of Stalingrad, which our intervention in Siberia undoubtedly brought about, the Germans finally overcame Russian resistance, and in the spring of 1943 came a negotiated peace, with the result that could have been expected. Stalin's régime did not survive the draconian terms imposed by Hitler, who enforced upon the Russians the same kind of peace he had made with the French in 1940.

Our Russian campaign, and the triumph of the Axis in Europe, radically shifted—for ever—the balance of world power. The next step was predictable: the 'realists' in America stepped forward, and forced a change of government. American

industrial and military circles saw that America had nothing to
hope for from a Britain in the throes of losing her Empire,
and unlikely ever to return to a Europe now firmly under Nazi
rule. They looked for a strong man, with proven authoritarian
tastes, able and willing to use military power to repress popular
discontent. A general had been found in the past perfectly
willing to use force to break up ex-servicemen's protest marches
in Washington. He had since been a proconsul in the Philippines, and was brought back: Douglas MacArthur.

In theory, all had gone well. We had, between us, restored a
world of military order and authority, broken Bolshevism,
reduced the old colonial empires to dust. If interests had continued to preside over the fate of the world, we could have built
upon that basis. But when you are dealing with passions,
interests give way. That is what we found with Germany. Was
it not the old Field-Marshal Yamagata who said with great
foresight that sooner or later Japan would find herself leading
the non-white races of the world in a struggle against the white
races? When the day comes, he said in 1914, that the great
conflict in Europe is over (he was one war too early, but the
general lines of the prediction stand), 'the rivalry between the
white and the non-white races will become violent, and who can
say that the white races will not unite with one another to
oppose the coloured peoples?'

How right he was. We had helped to establish a strong
government in the USA, on the assumption that anti-
communism would be the basis for an alliance between us. But
once the USSR was defeated, the racial basis of right-wing
America showed itself. There was first harassment, then
segregation, and finally, by 1945, the establishment of concentration camps for the coloured peoples of the USA, and the
Japanese in California and Hawaii were the targets of that
policy.

And it had a backer. Hitler had never had any love for us,
and I never shared Oshima's conviction that our future lay with
the Nazi regime. It was a matter of expediency, not of ideology.
But that is where passion came in, and drove interest out. The

MacArthur government reached out and took Hitler by the hand. Some of our generals had been foolish enough to boast about going on to the Urals after a pause for breath at the Yenisei, and there were some in Hitler's entourage who used those rumours to arouse in the Führer the old Yellow Peril theme. Racial passion is beyond the reach of reason, and it is beyond the reach even of self-interest. When I think back to the days of 1939 and 1940, a military alliance between the USA and Germany must have seemed the most absurd nonsense. Then, there it was, staring us in the face. The Nazis' immense Panzer legions, made up of the masses of Eastern Europe officered by German tank commanders, burst across the steppes. The Americans had carrier fleets moving out from the Aleutians and Pearl Harbor and—in a secret and lightning stroke—destroyed Yamamoto's great Combined Fleet in the seas between Japan and Hawaii. Their light bombers, flying from specially constructed aircraft carriers, made havoc of our cities, as the Germans approached Manchuria.

I think it was that bombing which pushed me into the last desperate throw. Some of our scientists had developed a new type of bomb, based on a theory developed by the British scientist Rutherford in the 1930s, which would multiply the force of an explosion to an incomparably greater magnitude than any other bomb known. We had physicists in Japan who could work on such developments—there was a Professor Nishina who explained the theory to me, but I was concerned with the results, not the ideas. When I saw Tokyo and Osaka ablaze after the first American raids, I had no hesitation in recommending the use of counter-terror. They say I destroyed San Francisco and Los Angeles without any possibility of distinguishing between civilian and military targets—but they had not seen the fire-storms in the Japanese cities. If we had had more such bombs, I would have used them, but the first two exhausted the industrial capacity we had allocated to making them. Before we could make more, the Germans were in Korea, ready to land in a Japan that was half-incinerated anyway. So I cannot blame those who removed me. My policy of realism had served my Emperor, I believed—and still believe. I did not reckon on the combined strength of tyranny and race.

I did, of course, expect the Americans to use me as an example. I had ordered the bombs to be dropped, so my trial was a bare formality, though it is hypocritical of the German and American prosecutors to claim that the use of nuclear weapons puts Japan beyond the pale. What would they have done in my shoes?

They might at least remove the manacles. The way these hand-cuffs are fastened to the band round my body makes it impossible to move my arms properly. And why do they insist that I die in these rags? When my *samurai* ancestors went to their last battle—they usually knew—they wore their very best clothes, and perfumed their helmets with incense. I am going to my death wearing US Army fatigues, with my shirt sticking out of my trousers, and that huge 'P' on the back. Do they really suppose I am likely to escape?

Ah, they will remove the manacles so that we can leave our signatures with Hanayama. Good thick Japanese paper, and the brush. And I can light the incense stick to make an offering. I'm pleased to see that they've allowed Hanayama to share a cup of wine with us. I asked for that specially. Two minutes to go. Hanayama is reading the *Sutra of the Three Promises*. I think he knows that for me, now, it is superfluous. I told him, a few hours ago, 'when it comes to the final reckoning, the chanting of the Sacred Name, and this alone, is enough.'

Hanayama will need other things to pass on to my family. I've taken out my dentures, and he'd better have my spectacles, too. Hair and nail clippings. And of course my prayer beads.

The duty officer takes us from the Buddhist chapel, with the German and the American chaplains and Hanayama just behind him. Hanayama shakes us all by the hand at the door of the gallows, and gives us his blessing. 'Thank you for everything you have done for us,' I said to him. 'Look after our families.'

So we go through the door. It is one minute past midnight. Namu Amida Butsu. Namu Amida Butsu. Namu Amida ...

3

Could Tojo's speculations ever have become reality? Everything that I have quoted about him, or from him, other than his own 'futurizing' (which begins on page 148) is absolute fact, so perhaps the reader can decide. On the central issue, whether or not America and Great Britain could have been divided by adroit Japanese diplomacy, the answer is probably No. At least by 1941. Earlier than that, I'm not so sure. Denny's book, which no one seems to read these days, has some very convincing arguments about the economic warfare already existing between Britain and the USA in the 1930s. The wartime alliance, and the good—but fluctuating—relations ever since, have made us look upon the present links as inevitable. But unthinkable switches can be made, either for temporary advantage like the 1939 Nazi-Soviet Pact, or the dissolution of the centuries-old Franco-German hostility which appears to be going on now. America's first war was with the British. There was certainly a risk of hostilities during the Civil War. And in 1956, at the time of Suez, the relations between Eden and Dulles showed an alliance that was certainly wearing thin at the edges. But in the throes of its militarist adventure in China in 1937 and 1938, Japan was in no mood to sound out the possibility of separating the vital interests of Britain and America; and after that the Japanese were not in a good position to try.

Would the US have intervened had Japan not attacked British and US possessions directly, but simply made for Java with a seaborne expedition? American public opinion was certainly reluctant to go to war. In his autobiography, *A Long Row of Candles*, Cy Sulzberger of *The New York Times* quotes the one-time Secretary of State, Byrnes, as saying that if Roosevelt had attempted to declare war on Japan, on the very eve of Pearl Harbor, he would have been opposed by two-thirds of Congress. On the other hand, Herbert Feis points out (in *The Road to Pearl Harbor*, pp. 303–4) that the President had been advised by his Chiefs of Staff, General Marshall and Admiral Stark, on November 5, 1941, that war should be avoided— unless Japan attacked or threatened directly territories whose security was 'of very great importance' to the United States. British Empire territory and the Netherlands East Indies *were* included in this category. The US cabinet believed, according to Feis, that the American people would support the Administration if it struck at Japan in the event the Japanese attacked British or Dutch territory in the Pacific. We have no means of testing whether it was a justifiable belief or not. Pearl Harbor put an end to those questions once and for all.

I have used fact in one or two other instances, but differently from what occurred. Richard Sorge, for example, *did* warn the Russians that Japan intended to move south, and that it was therefore safe for the Russians to assume, in 1941 and 1942, that they could move troops from the Far East. It is likely that this tipped the scales at Stalingrad, and hence had a decisive effect on the war in Europe. Sorge was in fact arrested by the Japanese police on October 17, 1941—some of his Japanese colleagues in espionage having been pulled in a few days earlier.

It is certainly true that a sizeable proportion of Japan's officer corps viewed the Soviet Union as the real enemy. Japanese troops had been in occupation of part of the Russian Far Eastern territories until 1921, as part of the general Allied effort to contain the Russian Revolution; and in 1939 war had broken out on quite a large scale between Russians and Japanese on the Manchurian border, where the Japanese had been severely mauled.

It is also true that interests closely linked to the Japanese Army used two missionary priests, Father Drought and Father Walsh of the Maryknoll Fathers, to make approaches to the US government other than through the State Department, where it was felt (rightly) that anti-Japanese influence was

solidly entrenched. The priests did in fact use their influence
with Roosevelt's Postmaster General, Frank Walker, to convey
the views of certain Japanese Army circles, and they were
accompanied by a Colonel Iwakuro who went on to achieve
fame as the leader of an Imperial Guards Tank Regiment in the
campaign against Singapore, was instrumental in running a
renegade army of Indian troops against the British, and later
in life, in post-war academic retirement, debated the future of
nationalism with Arnold Toynbee in the columns of the
Japanese press.

It might, of course, seem fantastic to switch round the dropping
of the first atomic bombs. But the Japanese were fairly advanced
in atomic physics, and when their scientists were flown to
examine the damage and casualties in Hiroshima in August
1945, they knew almost at once what kind of bomb had been
used. It has recently been suggested that they were in fact
working on a similar device, though the evidence for this seems
to be very slight. On the other hand, by 1947 or 1948, when I
imagine it happening . . . ?

NOTES

1 The *jūshin*: elder statesmen who advised on the selection of the Premier.

2 The American cryptographer, Herbert Yardley, published in 1931 *The American Black Chamber*, in which he gave an account of successful code-breaking, including penetration of the Japanese codes. In translation, the book became a Japanese best-seller.

BIBLIOGRAPHY

On Tojo, consult: Robert J. C. Butow, *Tojo and the coming of war* (Stanford University Press, 1961).
Courtney Browne, *Tojo: The Last Banzai* (Holt Rinehart and Winston, New York, 1967).

On the Far East War Crimes Trials: Richard H. Minear, *Victor's Justice. The Tokyo War Crimes Trial* (Princeton University Press, 1971).
On the background: Louis Allen, *Japan: The Years of Triumph* (MacDonald, London, 1971).
Richard Storry, *A History of Modern Japan* (Penguin Books, 1960).

If I had been . . .

KONRAD ADENAUER IN 1952

'How I would have accepted Stalin's proposal for a united neutralized Germany.'

ROGER MORGAN

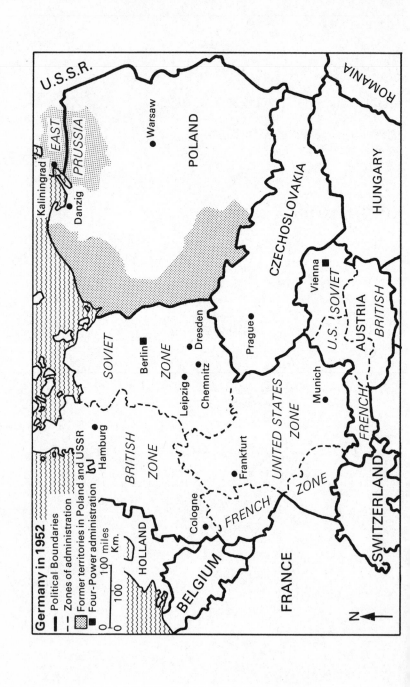

Germany in 1952
- Political Boundaries
- Zones of administration
- Former territories in Poland and USSR
- Four-Power administration

1

*In March 1952, seven years after the Unconditional Surrender
of Germany and three years after the occupying powers had set
up two rival German states—the Federal Republic in the West
and the German Democratic Republic in the East—the Western
allies were approaching a fundamental decision about Germany's
future. Under the impact of the Korean War in 1950 and the
growing tension of the Cold War throughout the world, the
Americans had taken the lead in pressing for the Federal Republic
to be rearmed and brought into the North Atlantic Treaty
Organization (NATO). Despite some hesitation, in Britain and
especially in France, as well as reluctance by large sectors of West
German opinion to give up the post-war idea of Germany's
demilitarization, the German Chancellor Konrad Adenauer led
his country and his allies firmly along the path towards German
rearmament. It was agreed that in May the Federal Republic and
the Western allies would sign treaties making West Germany a
full partner in the Western alliance, and also committing her to
make a substantial military contribution by joining a new European Defence Community (to be part of NATO) with France
and four other continental countries.*

*At this point, on March 10, 1952, the Soviet government under
Stalin (who was to remain in power until his death a year later)
made a dramatic proposal. In notes to the American, British and
French governments, Stalin called for the signing of a peace
treaty between all the wartime allies and the government of a*

reunified and independent Germany. The Soviet notes suggested the removal of all foreign military forces and bases from Germany within a year of the treaty's coming into force, and called for full democratic rights for all political forces in Germany, except those opposed to democracy and the cause of peace. The Soviet plan also provided for Germany's neutrality and required her not to enter 'any coalition or military alliance directed against any state which participated in the war against Germany'. The reunified Germany would be allowed to build up such land, air and sea forces as were necessary for her own defence (though German production of military material would be limited), and would be helped to become a member of the United Nations.

The Western leaders, including Adenauer, decided that these proposals were a tactical manoeuvre, designed to obstruct the development of West Germany's links with the West and especially her rearmament. Stalin's proposal was rejected. Although the Social Democratic opposition in West Germany, led by the veteran politician Kurt Schumacher, argued that the Soviet proposal offered a real hope of national reunification, and should be taken seriously, Adenauer and the allied governments decided to take no chances, and to press ahead with the rearmament of West Germany as if the Soviet note had never been sent. The treaties bringing West Germany into the alliance were signed at the end of May 1952, as planned, and after a further period of difficult discussions between the Western governments—including the abandonment of the original European Defence Community plan in 1954—the Federal Republic became a full member of NATO in May 1955.

Adenauer was bitterly criticized in Germany and abroad for his decision not to explore the Russian proposals for German reunification, but he continued to argue, until his retirement in 1963 and his death four years later, that the neutralization of Germany between East and West was too high a price for reunification, since a neutralized Germany would have risked political instability at home and Russian domination from abroad. Germany has remained divided into two states down to the present day.

2

Extract from Konrad Adenauer, *Memoirs*, 1966.

The Western allies' first reaction to the Soviet note was strongly negative: they saw in Stalin's proposal no more than a tactical device, aimed at disrupting our plans for the Federal Republic's rearmament as a member of the Western alliance. On the day after the publication of the Soviet note, March 11, the allied governments informed me through their High Commissioners: 'We shall continue with our negotiations on the European Defence Community and the German Treaty as if the note did not exist.'

I responded by saying that though their reaction to the Soviet note was probably justified, it might be unwise and premature to reject Stalin's proposals without exploring the prospect they offered of solving the problem of Germany's division. By the time I met the three High Commissioners on March 17 for a detailed discussion of the Soviet note, I had worked out in detail my reasons for believing that it should be taken with some seriousness. The French High Commissioner François-Poncet, his British colleague Sir Ivone Kirkpatrick, and the American General Hays, deputizing for High Commissioner McCloy, listened in silence as I expounded my views on the sort of reply which I suggested their governments ought to make.

In my judgement there were five main reasons why the Western powers, in close consultation with myself, should give serious consideration to the Soviet proposals. It was not easy for me to adopt this approach, since I was well aware of the powerful counter-arguments and had no love for Stalin. But after careful reflection I was convinced by the weight of each one of these five points.

First, and most important, Stalin appeared to be offering a solution to the most burning and fundamental problem of Germany, that of reunification. Under the immediate impact of the collapse of the Third Reich in 1945, the German people had been prepared to accept the division of their country into zones of allied military occupation. They had been too preoccupied by the task of rebuilding the shattered cities to try to resist the fact that the British, French, American and Soviet occupation authorities were pursuing different policies, and that by 1949 the Soviet Zone had been declared a separate 'workers' and peasants' state' in which eighteen million Germans were subjected to the rule of the Soviet puppets Ulbricht and Grotewohl. In any case, how could the division have been resisted? The Germans in the West could condemn the actions of Ulbricht and his Soviet masters, but their condemnation went hand in hand with a realization of their impotence to prevent what was happening.

By 1952, however—seven years after the end of the war—it seemed clear to me that the urge of the German people for reunification was a force which would continue to grow until it destroyed all the obstacles in its path. The impulse towards national unity, which had almost triumphed in 1848, had lain dormant only for a brief period before it produced the unified *Reich* under Bismarck in 1870. As I knew from my personal experience of political life since the turn of the century, the concept of German unity was powerful enough to overcome even the most daunting obstacles. In the Versailles Treaty of 1919, France had tried to set back the clock by detaching parts of Germany's territory and giving them to Poland, as well as by placing Danzig and the Saarland under the League of Nations, and by banning the union of Germany and Austria which both peoples ardently desired: within a very few years Hitler, borne to power on a tide of national resentment against these French policies, had torn up the Versailles Treaty and re-established the unity of the *Reich*. It was clear to me by 1952 that, just as the Germans had refused to tolerate Versailles, so they would not indefinitely put up with the new partition of their country between Russia and the Western powers, the handing over of East Prussia to the Poles and Königsberg to the Soviet Union, and the renewed occupation of the Saarland by France.

Already the German people were strongly attracted to the

arguments of political spokesmen who gave urgent priority to the goal of reunification, in particular the opposition leader Dr Kurt Schumacher, of the Social Democratic Party, and also Dr Thomas Dehler, the leader of the Free Democratic Party. The growing popularity of these men, it seemed to me, made it a certainty that if national reunification were not achieved soon, the Germans would turn to more extreme leaders, as they had turned to Hitler in 1933, who would achieve what the Germans wanted but only at a terrible cost. It was better, in my opinion, that the possibility of reunification, held out by Stalin's note, should be firmly pursued by a responsible statesman such as myself, rather than becoming the vehicle for a new demagogue in the model of Hitler.

My first reason for taking up Stalin's offer, therefore, was my conviction that the reunification of our country under democratic leaders was the only way, in the longer run, to hold at bay the more extreme political forces which I well knew Germany could produce, and to guide the energies of the Germans into constructive and moderate channels.

My second reason, which followed directly from this, was my judgement that there would be considerable political rewards for the party which could claim the credit for restoring national unity. Many of my colleagues in the Christian Democratic Union, particularly those from Southern and Western Germany, were afraid that free elections throughout a reunited Germany, as proposed by Stalin, would be certain to give a majority to the Social Democratic Party, and for this reason urged me not to consider accepting the Soviet proposal. I knew, of course, that the major cities of the so-called German Democratic Republic— Dresden, Leipzig, and Berlin itself—had traditionally voted for the Social Democrats: indeed, I knew this better than anyone, because for most of my first period as Mayor of Cologne, from 1917 to 1933, I had been obliged to deal with an almost-permanent Social Democratic majority government in power in Berlin, the capital of Prussia. Dr Schumacher and his colleagues in the Social Democratic Party were certainly motivated in their constant demand for reunification by their belief that in the parliament of a reunified Germany they would be the largest party, rather than being slightly weaker than the Christian Democratic majority elected to the West German Bundestag in 1949.

My own assessment of the likely outcome of all-German elections, however, was different. I had several reasons for believing that the voters in the Eastern part of Germany, once the moment came for free elections, would desert their traditional Social Democratic allegiance and give massive support to the Christian Democratic Union. The Left had been discredited in the so-called German Democratic Republic, far more than Dr Schumacher and his party colleagues realized, by the forced incorporation of the Social Democrats, under their treacherous leader Otto Grotewohl, into the Socialist Unity Party dominated by the Communist Ulbricht and his Soviet masters. The Christian Democratic Union also had a much broader appeal than had been possible for the old Centre Party before 1933, since it embraced Protestants as well as the Centre Party's Catholics: this was an immense factor of strength for us in the Protestant areas of East Germany. In any case, it was clear to me that the party which grasped the opportunity to reunify Germany could be sure of a huge advantage in the gratitude of the German people: every day brought new evidence of the longing of the Germans for the reunion of their nation— almost every family in the Federal Republic was separated from relatives in the East—and the gratitude of these millions of Germans represented a political prize which I was determined to win for my party. The first elections to the all-German Reichstag, as I shall describe later, were to prove me right to an extent which even I had not anticipated.

My third reason for deciding to take up the Soviet offer of reunification was that it held a clear-cut alternative to the political federation of Western Europe—it was unthinkable that the Russians would allow a unified Germany to join a Western-oriented bloc of this kind—and by 1952 European federation looked an infinitely remote and even utopian prospect. It was true that in the first years after Germany's collapse in 1945 the glowing ideal of merging the national identities of Germans, French, Belgians and Italians into a United States of Europe had held great fascination—not least to the Germans, whose position after 1945 was that of a material bankrupt and a moral outcast. Many Germans, indeed, including my senior diplomatic adviser Professor Walter Hallstein, were deeply committed to the belief that Germany could be saved from the daemonic temptations of her past—especially the temptation to play off East against West, Russia against the allies—by binding herself indissolubly into the kind of federal Europe preached by the great Frenchman Jean Monnet. I personally had deep sympathy for this point of view, in theory: as a Rhinelander and a Catholic, I had always felt more drawn towards the west and the south of Europe—towards Paris and Lake Como—than towards the bleak plains of Protestant Prussia. However, as I looked at the state of Western Europe in March 1952, I could see little hope, in practice, of achieving the sort of European union which might provide a haven for the restless German soul. The Coal and Steel Community of the Six, it is true, was just starting its operations from a modest headquarters in Luxemburg, under the able presidency of Jean Monnet. But coal and steel, however great their importance, were not enough in themselves to signify the arrival of a United States of Europe, either today or in the near future. In Great Britain, the new Conservative government of Winston Churchill was just as strongly opposed as the Labour government of Clement Attlee to British membership, either of the Coal and Steel Community or of the European Defence Community which France had proposed as a framework for the rearmament of the Federal Republic.

Faced with this British insularity, the French government itself—or rather a long series of short-lived ones—had begun to hesitate profoundly about its own commitment to European unity. There were alarming signs that the anti-European forces in French politics were gaining the upper hand: the elections of 1951 had brought great strength not only to the Communists but also to the followers of General de Gaulle, who were implacably opposed to the surrender of French sovereignty implied by the proposed European Defence Community. In this situation it seemed most unwise to me to place excessive faith in the concept of European union as a goal for German policy, and much more prudent to give priority to the cause of national reunification, which corresponded to the real needs and aspirations of the German people. This was a further factor indicating that Stalin's offer should be actively pursued.

Fourthly, there was the difficult question of the relationship which would develop between a reunified, internationally neutral Germany and the Soviet bloc.

The pessimists argued that a neutral Germany would be dangerously weak in the face of Soviet pressure, and would quickly become totally subordinate to Soviet influence. They also argued (somewhat inconsistently) that, from the point of view of Poland, Hungary, and the other Soviet satellites, a reunified Germany would be an over-powerful and therefore threatening neighbour, and that this would make good relations impossible. I was convinced, after careful reflection, that these contrasting images, of a weak Germany subject to Soviet influence, and a Germany too powerful to develop good relations with its smaller Eastern neighbours, were both wrong.

It seemed to me that a German government with a clear sense of what it could and could not do, and a determined will to preserve the country's independence, would certainly be able to resist domination by the Soviet Union. The Russians, after all, were offering to make an important concession by withdrawing from their own zone of occupation, and their proposed peace treaty explicitly allowed Germany to maintain the military forces necessary for its defence. This was a good start for a future German government, and moreover a German statesman who knew how to exploit the international balance of power skilfully and with moderation would have a number of other resources at his disposal. For instance, it was clear that the United States would keep a watchful eye on developments in Germany, and that any attempt by the Russians to exert undue pressure on the government in Berlin could be countered by the German Chancellor discreetly mobilizing American pressure on Moscow. Even if the Russians did attempt to intervene in Germany's internal affairs—for instance, by arguing that certain political parties were not, as their note put it, 'democratic', or 'peace-loving'—they could quickly be made to realize that pressures of this kind would only provoke an anti-Soviet reaction by the German people, and that by driving Germany into the arms of the Americans, the Russians would lose all the advantages they had gained by Germany's neutralization.

By 1952 I had been conducting the Federal Republic's foreign relations for long enough to have a good sense of how to deal with the Russian mentality, and I was confident that I could find the right arguments to maintain the independence of a united Germany against both Moscow and the supporters of the world Communist movement inside Germany. I did not forget how easily I had won the support of the Communist members of the Cologne City Council almost thirty years earlier, when I had put forward plans to build an expensive new bridge across the Rhine, by praising the beauty of Leningrad with its new bridge across the Neva!

As for the argument that Poland, Czechoslovakia, and the other small states in Central and Eastern Europe would be alarmed by the power of a reunited Germany, and that their fears would prevent the scheme from being implemented, I realized of course that this question required careful handling. I could see that it was essential for the new Germany to re-nounce, once and for all, any claim to the German territories taken by the Poles and Czechs, and even Russians, at the end of the Second World War. This would be a bitter pill for the German refugees from the lost areas to swallow: it was certain that the leader of the Refugee Party, Dr Seebohm, would resign from my cabinet, and it was not only the refugees from East Prussia who would have difficulty, as the Social Democrat Professor Carlo Schmidt expressed it, in accepting the idea that the great German philosopher Immanuel Kant had been born not in Königsberg but in Kaliningrad! However, I was confident that even the refugees from the East would realize the need to pay this price for the much greater benefit of unifying the German people—the eighteen million of the Soviet Zone with the fifty million of the Federal Republic—and would in time be reconciled to giving up their claims to their ancestral homelands.

In return for this assurance that Germany was not a threat, I was confident that the peoples of Eastern and Central Europe would warmly welcome the idea that Germany would be re-unified and free to develop more active relations with them. For one thing, there was their pressing need to liberate themselves from the one-sided pressure of the Soviet Union by getting themselves into a substantial relationship, both economic and political, with an important partner in the West. The Federal Republic, through its dynamic economy and its historical links with Central Europe, was in many ways the natural partner for these countries. It was in fact remarkable, as I was told by many visitors from Hungary, Poland, and other so-called 'peoples' democracies', that the historical links between Germany and her Eastern neighbours had survived the Third Reich and all that Hitler's regime had meant for Central Europe as a whole. Even though the Jewish intelligentsia, the main representatives of German culture in the Danubian states, had been destroyed or driven into emigration by the Third Reich, and even though other 'bourgeois' elements in the population had been forced to emigrate to the West after 1945, it was striking that German was still the main Western language used by leading circles in those countries, and that Germany was still regarded as their natural producer of advanced technological equipment.

Against this background I was confident that a reunified Germany, under moderate leadership, would be regarded as a friend rather than a threat by our Eastern neighbours, and that they would welcome our positive response to the settlement proposed by Stalin rather than seeing it as a matter for concern.

My fifth and final reason for reacting positively to the Soviet proposal was my judgement that the Western allies, although they would initially be alarmed by this change of direction in

Germany's policy, would on reflection find that the reunification and the neutralization of Germany were in their own interests as well as ours. In the United States, it was true, the strongly anti-Soviet policy of Secretary of State Acheson had triumphed over the more conciliatory views advanced by George Kennan and other members of the State Department's Policy Planning Staff, but 1952 was an election year, and it was significant that the Democratic Party's candidate, Adlai Stevenson, regarded Kennan as one of his main advisers on foreign policy questions. It was therefore very likely that the European policy advocated by Kennan in 1949, which included the evacuation of Germany by all the occupying powers, and the subsequent neutralization of the country, would become the policy of the new Administration. Even if the Republican candidate should win, there was good reason to think that the reunification and neutralization of Germany would be welcome to the American Administration and Congress, since the evacuation of America's massive occupation forces would represent a great saving both to the United States budget and also to the balance of payments. I also knew that the American government, which had very good relations with Belgium and the Netherlands, as well as with Great Britain, would be able to maintain substantial military forces in these countries, which would be near enough to reoccupy Western Germany in the event of a crisis, even in the event of anti-American forces coming to dominate the political scene in France, and obliging the Americans to withdraw the NATO headquarters and all their bases from France.

I was therefore sure that a positive response to Stalin's proposal would—even though after some debate—be acceptable to the United States. As for Great Britain and France, they also would obviously hesitate before abandoning their firm hold on their respective zones in Germany in favour of the uncertain prospects of a neutralized and reunified Germany. As with the United States, however, I was sure that the governments of London and Paris would, after some reflection, see the advantages of accepting Stalin's offer. The British, by 1952, were beginning to realize that their balance-of-payments problems were not merely a transitory effect of the Second World War, but reflected a deep-seated weakness in their economy and in their ability to face international competition. They knew that the military occupation of the British Zone represented an expense which they could not afford to keep up indefinitely, especially as German resistance to meeting the costs of stationing British forces was likely to mount as the years went by. It was therefore logical for the British to limit their commitments, and to welcome a political solution to the German problem which would allow the withdrawal of the British Army of the Rhine without any loss of face.

As for France, there was, I could see, the traditional fear of a German nation of whom the great statesman Clemenceau had said 'the only trouble with the Germans is that there are twenty million too many of them'. This justified fear of German domination had to be met by firm guarantees, first, that Germany's rearmament would be strictly limited to her defensive needs; secondly, that France's economic union with the Saar territory would be preserved, even if the Saarland were to become politically part of the Federal Republic, as its population wished; and thirdly, that Germany would enter into economic arrangements with France which would guarantee French agricultural produce a preferential access to the German market, on financial terms to be subsidized by the German taxpayer.

It seemed to me that if these considerations were satisfied, the Federal Republic would face no serious objections from her Western allies in embarking on the new direction in German history which the Soviet note of March 10, 1952 opened up to us.

The developments of the next few years were to prove my calculations essentially correct. There was of course no difficulty in gaining the support of the majority of the German people for my policy of coming to terms with the Soviet Union, once I had given a clear lead. The Germans were not only deeply relieved at the prospect of reunification (and incidentally at some other benefits such as the immediate repatriation of thousands of prisoners of war still in Russia); they also responded, as I knew they would, to the sense of national significance which the new position of Germany gave them. As the details of the settlement were worked out in the two years after Stalin's original note, it became clear that the neutralization of Germany, far from reducing her international status, marked a great improvement over the partition and military occupation of the years before 1952.

My calculation that the Christian Democratic Union, and myself as its leader, would reap the political rewards of our courage was, as we now know, amply borne out by the first all-German elections to the Berlin Reichstag in 1954. I knew that we had nothing to fear from the extreme Left: the Communist Party throughout Germany was of course deeply demoralized by the decision of Ulbricht, Grotewohl and the other leaders of the 'German Democratic Republic' to go into exile in Moscow when the agreement on reunification was reached, and it was no surprise that the Communists won only a handful of seats in the Reichstag. The critical question, of course, was whether the Social Democrats would be able to mobilize their old voting strength in Berlin and other cities of central Germany. The election campaign in these areas was a hard one, but by polling day it was clear that even old Social Democratic voters were transferring their support to the party which had given them the chance to vote in a reunified Germany. As history shows, the 1954 election brought large majorities for the Christian Democratic Union in the rural constituencies in Mecklenburgh and Thuringia. Our greatest satisfaction, however, was our resounding victory over the Social Democrats in their former strongholds, the cities of Leipzig, Dresden, Chemnitz, and of course Berlin itself.

My massive majority in the 1954 Reichstag put me in a strong position to proceed with the remaining details of the new arrangements. It will be recalled that I had anticipated the argument that a reunified and neutralized Germany would be incompatible with the economic and political integration of

Western Europe, to which we had been committed since the late 1940s. When I put the issue squarely to our French and British partners, and asked for their assessments of how fast they themselves were prepared to move towards European union, they were forced to admit the deep reservations which I had already detected, and to accept that the nebulous prospect of a united Europe could not be allowed to hold up concrete steps towards the reunification of Germany. It was easy to work out economic arrangements which were beneficial to all concerned—similar to those between the West European countries and neutralized Austria—but the political design for a United States of Europe was very reasonably postponed until the distant future, perhaps for ever. As I discussed these arrangements with Churchill and with the new French Prime Minister Mendès-France in the summer of 1954, I formed a strong impression that they were deeply grateful to me for putting the concept of European integration into a more realistic perspective for all concerned.

My calculations about Germany's Eastern neighbours proved to be correct too. After some hard bargaining in the early stages of the negotiations about the political activities to be allowed in reunified Germany, and about the permitted level of German rearmament, the Soviet Union quickly modified its position. I had expected this, as the main objective of German neutralization was of such fundamental importance from the Russian point of view. There have, of course, been moments of friction with Moscow since the agreements came into effect, but a combination of firmness and moderation has allowed me, as I expected, to preserve Germany's independent and neutral position. It has also proved relatively easy to allay the fears of our smaller Eastern neighbours about the possible risk of German domination. Our clear acceptance of the frontiers of 1945, although it was very painful for the refugees, has made it possible to develop the very positive economic relations in Central and Eastern Europe which I anticipated in 1952.

One of my main problems in 1952 was of course to win the

support of the three Western powers for the radical change in policy I wished to make. I knew even before my meeting with the High Commissioners on March 17 that I should have to face difficult arguments with Washington, London and Paris. Before long, however, my assessment of the balance of thinking in the allied capitals had been proved correct—it helped at a critical moment that the new President Eisenhower early in 1953 was keen to appear as the bringer of a peace settlement in Germany, as well as in Korea—and I could count on strong Western support for my plan.

In retrospect I can fairly say that my decision in 1952 to accept German reunification on Stalin's terms has changed the course of European history. Instead of the sterile confrontation between two hostile German states, which might have had grave consequences in perpetuating the Cold War between East and West, Europe and the world have seen how a reunified, neutralized, and stable Germany can live at peace with itself and with its neighbours.

3

The above version of Adenauer's memoirs has nothing in common with the original (Konrad Adenauer, *Erinnerungen 1953–55*, Stuttgart, 1966), except that in both versions he *does* meet the Allied High Commissioners on March 17. The arguments we see him advancing in the above version are, of course, the direct opposite of the line he took in reality, but it is not implausible, in terms of his character and his view of politics, the he should have argued as he does here.

If Adenauer had in fact said 'yes' to Stalin's proposal, and convinced his allies that this was the right course, Germany's development in the last quarter of a century would certainly have been very different, and so would Europe's. The Berlin Wall would not have been built in 1961, Willy Brandt's attempt to bring the two German states closer together in the early 1970s would have been unnecessary, and the European Community could certainly not have developed as it has.

'How I would have accepted Stalin's proposal' assumes judgements and decisions both by Adenauer and by the Western allies which are most improbable, but not totally implausible. The choice we see Adenauer making here *was* advocated not only by Kennan but by Schumacher and other Germans too, and plans which went at least a small way in this direction were put forward by British statesmen of the time, including both Eden and Gaitskell. It did not happen, but it might have done.

If I had been . . .

ALEXANDER DUBCEK IN 1968

'How I would have saved the "Prague Spring" and prevented the Warsaw Pact invasion.'

PHILIP WINDSOR

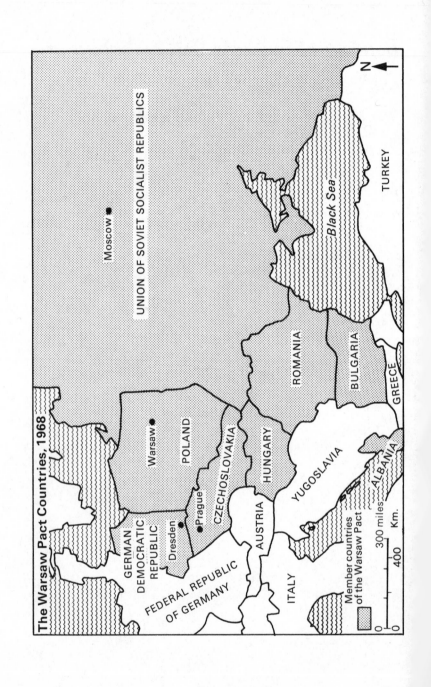

The Warsaw Pact Countries, 1968

1

Czechoslovakia, 1968. January: a new government is formed under Alexander Dubcek. August: the country is invaded by the forces of the Soviet Union and four other members of the Warsaw Pact. The months between had become known as the Prague Spring, an extraordinary period of growing hope and freedom. This is how events developed.

Dubcek replaced a harsh and increasingly discredited ruler, Antonin Novotny, whose last months in office were marked by economic crisis, social tension, and nationalist strains between Czechs and Slovaks. The signs are that the new government was acceptable to the Russians, who were themselves anxious to see a measure of economic reform. They probably thought of Dubcek as a relatively amenable figure who would not risk antagonizing the bosses in the Kremlin. For all that was really known of him was that he had been quite a successful First Secretary of the Party in Slovakia, that he had been well trained from early youth in Communist politics, and that for a Party official of some standing he was a modest and unassuming character. Nobody could have expected—perhaps not even Dubcek himself—that he would now try to create a new form of socialism altogether.

But he did. Already by March, his new style of government—which he had characterized as that of 'socialism with a human face'—was causing concern to the other members of the Warsaw Pact. Yet the expression of this concern, at a Pact meeting in Dresden, did not prevent the publication, in April, of the govern-

ment's *Action Programme, which aroused great enthusiasm inside Czechoslovakia. By the early summer, press censorship, though never officially abolished was allowed to lapse.*

Clearly, these developments set alarm bells ringing in the other Communist countries, particularly East Germany, whose Party boss, Walter Ulbricht, was demanding from an early date that the Soviet government should put an end to the Czechoslovak reforms. Dubcek was on occasion summoned to Moscow to account for himself. In June, after considerable pressure on the government in Prague, Soviet forces entered Czechoslovakia on manoeuvres, which were officially scheduled to last three weeks, but in fact dragged on until the beginning of August. In the meantime, in July, at another meeting of the Warsaw Pact in Warsaw, a threatening letter was delivered to the Czechoslovak delegation, warning it to mend its ways. But at the same time at home, a manifesto of leading writers and intellectuals, called Two Thousand Words, *pledged support to the government and called upon it to resist Soviet pressure and create the conditions for full democracy. Finally, the Soviet forces around the borders of Czechoslovakia were reinforced and placed on alert. In the shadow thrown by this massive mobilization, Dubcek and other members of his government met Brezhnev and other leaders of the Warsaw Pact in two conferences at the beginning of August. In return for an undertaking that the Party in Prague would exercise greater control and remain in command of the country, the other powers promised not to interfere in its internal affairs. Dubcek kept to his undertaking—but in a way which must have startled the Russians even more than anything he had done so far. On August 10, a new constitution for the Party was put forward in Czechoslovakia which was intended to open it to democratic scrutiny. In other words, the Party might continue to control the country, but it would now become an assembly of citizens, not that instrument of dictatorial power from which Dubcek had been moving away for the past eight months. The Soviet Union broke its promise: on August 21, its forces invaded.*

Dubcek and his lieutenants were taken off to Moscow, where they were humiliated and browbeaten, for a part of the time literally in chains. The Soviet leaders attempted to force their resignation, to make them abandon the programme of reform, to accept the permanent presence of Soviet forces in their country. On this third point, they had no choice; but on the first two they refused. And after a few days, to universal astonishment, they were allowed to return to Prague—still the government of the country.

In part, they were enabled to do so by the immense display of solidarity and resolve which was shown by the Czechoslovak people. Nothing had been organized beforehand, but a wave of spontaneous resistance swept the country. The demonstrations which became so famous on television were only the visible form of what was happening: indeed, the fact that Prague Television was able to transmit them at all showed how much ingenuity and improvised cooperation had gone into keeping the networks open. There was a quality of brilliance as well as bravery in the manner whereby journalists, cameramen, technicians, were able to switch from one transmitting station to another, evade Soviet searches and Soviet jamming attempts, and continue to provide a full account of what was happening. Similarly, railway workers acted together, without any previous planning, to confuse and misdirect the Soviet troop trains, and ensure that reinforcements did not reach places where they were most needed. The Soviet invasion had effectively prevented the meeting of a Party Congress, which Dubcek had scheduled for September. But in fact, many members of the Party did manage to get to a secret congress, in spite of the presence of half a million foreign troops in their country. Their resolution, too, demonstrated the commitment they brought to the ideal of socialism with a human face.

In the end, of course, the Russians won. The Prague Spring did survive into the autumn, at least in the sense that the government continued to prepare even more extensive reforms, but during the winter it was extinguished. One by one, the most impressive leaders of Czechoslovakia were ousted by Soviet pressure. Finally in April 1969, Alexander Dubcek was forced to resign.

A peculiarly bitter irony was to be found in the nature of his successor. He was Gustav Husak, a hero of the Slovak Rising of

1944 against the Nazi occupation. His record since that time had shown that such courage was not confined to the circumstances of war: in his defence of Slovak rights against the centralizing powers of Prague he incurred the wrath of Stalin and of the Czech Stalinist, Antonin Novotny, and had suffered severely in prison. He was also no mean intellectual. Many people, both inside and outside Czechoslovakia, hoped that this intellectual nationalist would be able, even while playing a game acceptable to the Russians, to salvage some measure of freedom and tolerance at home. But far from it. Czechoslovakia is today one of the most repressive countries in Eastern Europe, and Husak still runs it.

Well, could Dubcek have avoided all this? He was an immensely brave and very decent man, a symbol to millions of men and women. But was he a very good politician? Was he decisive at the wrong moments and indecisive at the right ones? Many people in his team urged him to act differently over important issues. What would have happened if he had? What would one have done in his place—supposing I had been Dubcek in 1968?

2

Of course, I don't really mean to talk as if I were literally Dubcek. If I had been that brave and trusting man in 1968, I would, obviously, have behaved just as he did. But nor do I mean if Dubcek had been me. That would presuppose that he had never been trained by the Comintern, had never helped to run the Party apparatus in Slovakia, had not brought with him 101 assumptions about the nature of Communist power which made the transformation of Czechoslovak society all the more astonishing.

What I do mean is a kind of historical transplant, in which I substitute some of the knowledge of what has happened since for some of the assumptions that he brought with him when he came to power in 1968. But in this transplant it is I who am free to reject some of Dubcek's own views, and free therefore to act differently.

But even before I do that, there is a certain difficulty. Alexander Dubcek was, as the Americans say, a very private person. Indeed, part of his immense appeal might have lain in the fact that, although he showed his feelings with extraordinary candour, he never sought to impose, and seldom spelled out, his political attitudes. This unassuming character enabled him to make direct contact with millions of his fellow citizens, but it doesn't make it easy to get a fix on the beliefs that he brought with him to power: so I shall have to take some of them for granted.

First, I presume that he didn't regard the Communist takeover in Czechoslovakia in 1948 as in any sense a coup—rather as the logical fulfilment of the political struggles inside the country over the previous three years, and indeed, of much of its history before the Nazi invasion. So he didn't feel the need to apologize for being a Communist. What was necessary was to achieve real socialism instead of fake socialism. In turn, this meant getting rid of the habits of Stalinism to which the previous rulers of Czechoslovakia had so tenaciously clung. After all Czechoslovakia had been very reluctant to de-Stalinize, and on more than one occasion it was Khrushchev's or Brezhnev's Russians who had given it a push. And so, in turn, it followed from this that it would be possible to liberalize Czechoslovak society in cooperation with the Soviet Union, and not against it. One could, in short, trust the Russians.

Now, I, the new *post facto* Dubcek, don't necessarily reject all this. Certainly, I agree there was no real coup in 1948. Certainly, if one held to one's beliefs, and, perhaps, above all, in private, it was possible to imagine that socialism could yet find a real meaning. It was even possible for someone like Dubcek to trust the Russians—so long as one only wanted to liberalize. But, of course, he very rapidly found that he wanted more. Within three months of coming to power he had committed himself to a programme, not of liberalization, but of democratization. The difference was fundamental.

Liberalization can be administered and then withdrawn. It comes in small doses, such as are necessary to keep the intellectuals quiet or get the economy moving. But when the need has passed, and production turns up, and the intellectuals are absorbed again, either into orthodoxy or into jail, why then the new boundaries have been established, and the system is still unchanged. It happens all over the place: Poland, East Germany, and even the Soviet Union itself.

Democratization is altogether different. It means allowing debate, and a perpetual momentum of debate. It means the constant exposure of those at the top to criticism from below; and the rendering of accounts about the use of power. And the Dubcek who was impelled, perhaps by the realization of his own inner potential, perhaps in response to those around him, to move from liberalization to democratization, never stopped to ask whether he could still trust the Russians.

But if I had been Dubcek I would certainly have done so! And, as no doubt he has had ample opportunity to reflect since then, he could have acted differently at many moments.

So let us imagine that we are in Czechoslovakia in April 1968 and that the government's Action Programme is about to be launched. On the face of it, this programme represents a fairly modest set of proposals: a new emphasis on the rights of Slovakia; a redefinition of the relations between party and government; and a sustained enquiry into the abuses of Stalinism. But its implications are enormous. The party is, at least potentially, beginning to limit its own power, and to open itself to scrutiny. And I, Dubcek, know that a majority of my governmental colleagues are now reforming radicals; they want to take it all farther. I have to hold a centrist position. For, after all, nearly half of them are still diehard conservatives. But I don't believe that I can out-manoeuvre them with the benevolent neutrality of the Russians. I should know that, from now on, the Russians are going to object, not merely to the pace, but also to the direction of any reforms in Czechoslovakia. The action programme might still look like liberalization, but anything further is democratization and, as such, would be dangerous stuff. So what do I do? I really have only two choices. The first is to play for time, and to try to control the pace of change. Or else I can try to bring things under control now. And this is what I decide to do.

In the Praesidium—effectively, in my cabinet—there are various voices urging me to hold a Party Congress as soon as possible. They argue that the longer it is delayed, the more radical it will be in context and demand. And the more radical it is, the more apprehensively the Russians will view it. The thing to do is convene it now, and to win the support of reformers in the party for a programme which, if it were held later, these reformers would emphatically reject as being inadequate. In this way, I can get the best of both worlds. I can reassert my control, and thereby please the Russians; because, after all, they prefer strong, efficient fellows to ineffective diehards. And, equally, I can get a new Central Committee and a new Praesidium elected, which will be dominated by centrists rather than radicals, and which I can expect to support me in a thoroughgoing overhaul of the economy.

So I send out instructions to get a Party Congress ready as a matter of urgency by the end of April or the beginning of May. There is already some bonus in this because the conservatives in the Praesidium do not want it. Naturally enough, the reformers therefore do. Both sides know that if the congress comes, the conservatives are finished. Perhaps not all the reformers yet appreciate, however, that by summoning the congress so soon, I am also helping to contain them for the future. There is more to the game of national politics than one may appreciate as First Secretary of the Party in Slovakia, which is roughly equivalent to being Secretary of State for Scotland. Now that I am First Secretary of the Party in the whole country, which is roughly equivalent to being Prime Minister, I can begin to enjoy it.

The Czechoslovak Communist Party is, and always has been, a comparatively large one. After all, it got 40 per cent of the vote in the last free elections. And the majority of members of this party will support me. But I also know that it is dominated, in district after district, organization after organization, by the worst elements—those who got preferment under Stalin and Novotny. I am going to change all this—now, before the Party Congress. There is a perfectly simple way of doing so—a purge. But not, of course, a purge on the 1937 model. There will be no Gulags in Czechoslovakia. All you do is re-register the entire membership of the Party. Everyone has to turn in his party card, and is then issued with a new one. Only, those to whom you take exception just do not get a new card and, therefore, cannot elect new delegates to the congress; and so the boys who brought in the vote until now will be excluded this time from any say at all.

The result is that I can hold my Party Congress at the beginning of May, with a sufficient degree of control to get rid of the Stalinist conservatives altogether. Even more important, perhaps, is the fact that I can now reassure the Russians. It has not escaped my notice, after all, that the first signs of real Soviet concern about my programme have appeared in Moscow in April. Already some Soviet generals are beginning to press for military action against my government and my country. I know that the Soviet government has been very reluctant to listen to them, and that the ruling trio certainly does not want an international crisis just now; but I am well aware that if developments in Czechoslovakia precipitate a crisis of confidence back in the Soviet Union, the Soviet leaders will not hesitate to put the boot in. My job is to help them avoid such a crisis. And the Congress has been a great help in this. It has demonstrated that the Party is in control of the country, and that I and my advisers are in control of the Party. My job now, making use as best I can of the leading role of the Party, is to demonstrate to the people of Czechsolovakia that I really mean that socialism will have a human face and, at the same time, demonstrate to the Russians that this will not threaten their system. In other words, I have to do the impossible. But I am going to try; and I am going to try, above all, by concentrating on the economic goals of my reform programme.

This means that many conventional ideas of liberty can still not be fully realized. The press is beginning to take the law into its own hands—acting as if censorship no longer existed. Of course, I hope that one day such a state of affairs can be achieved, but I also know that it would be foolish and dangerous to abolish censorship now. So, while I allow the office of censor to lapse, I institute what might be regarded as a kind of extended D-notice system. Editors are requested by the government not to print articles on a wide variety of sensitive subjects; notably, relations between Czechoslovakia and the Soviet Union, and the relations between party membership and administrative competence inside the country. On this basis of a relaxed, but still fairly well-controlled press, I try to win the mass support of the industrial workers.

My real task is to demonstrate that because of the mistakes in the past and the hopeless impasse to which centralized planning always reduces an economy, there is little tangible benefit to expect in the immediate future. But I also hope to demonstrate that, in a couple of years, things really will improve. The lectures which my deputy premier, Professor Ota Sik, has been giving on television have been a tremendous help. Indeed, one might reflect with some satisfaction that the Western countries, with their free trade unions and their demands for participation by the people in the government, have not yet between them produced anything like it. Could a Giscard d'Estaing or a Roy Jenkins really go on television and in a series of six unashamedly academic lectures on the nature of economics and the economy of their countries, secure not only a mass viewing audience, but also a very high degree of voluntary restraint in workers' demands for higher wages or better conditions?

But I am also bound to reflect that it takes a country where the Party is supposed to enjoy a monopoly of wisdom, and to hand down its understanding from on high, to produce such a phenomenon. In a sense, though, this merely confirms the rightness of my decisions. Humanism and reform must be brought to Czechoslovakia via the authority of the Party and not by abdicating from that authority. And I could also promise the workers rather more than a bit of economic advantage two years hence. I order work to be speeded up on the preparation of a law for workers' councils and workers' self-management in factories. In this way I intend to bring about the real participation of workers in the positions which affect them most closely—but to do so without abandoning the central authority of the Party in the state.

So, by the summer, what have I achieved? I have instituted a programme of economic reform; I have reformed the Party; I have maintained relations with the Soviet Union; and I have done all this without crisis. But now the Soviet Union has proposed that it should hold joint manoeuvres in Czechoslovakia with other Warsaw Pact forces during the month of June. Needless to say, I still don't trust the Russians. But I prepare an elaborately enthusiastic public welcome for the Soviet forces, and, even more important, announce in advance a farewell festival for a fixed date. The Russians don't trust me either, but, in the end, they find it difficult to drag the manoeuvres on without precipitating a sense of crisis; and so they depart with as much grace as they can muster.

Finally, in July, I have the chance to defend myself before the leaders of the fraternal parties of the socialist camp at a meeting in Warsaw. The appalling Herr Ulbricht brings with him from East Germany the draft of a letter to the Central Committee of the Czechoslovak Communist Party in which he talks about a situation which is 'absolutely unacceptable for a socialist country' and says that the 'basis of our ties and the security of the commonwealth of our countries are threatened'. Ulbricht, of course, cannot understand what is going on in Czechoslovakia, and nor can Brezhnev. In fact, the letter was probably drafted by Brezhnev for Ulbricht to put forward. But, because of the success I have achieved, it is comparatively easy for me to go to Warsaw and persuade the Russians that the letter is nonsense. At the end of the meeting, Brezhnev voices 'understanding' for the Praesidium of the Czechoslovak Communist Party in its attempt to carry out historically necessary reforms and strengthen socialism in the country.

It is at this point that I begin to have my doubts. These doubts, moreover, are shared by a number of Czechoslovak intellectuals and writers. What has happened to my experiment? How much farther can it really go? In moderating the pace have I not changed the direction? A clandestine letter is now circulating in Czechoslovakia, D-notice or no D-notice. This letter, untitled but generally known as *The 3,000 Words*, has made a profound analysis of the relationship between society, economics and the nature of truth; it has shown an uncanny ability to analyze what it calls 'Dubcek's hesitations' and my attempt to create a centrist framework for democratization on the instalment plan; it has declared that either one has the everyday quality of democracy or one hasn't. It makes it plain that I have let down those who had hoped and aspired with me at the beginning of the year. Socialism was not really creating humanism; it was simply becoming less brutal and more rational.

I now find myself obliged to reconsider my whole position. It is plain that my attempt to do things gradually and keep them under control could succeed only if it abandoned the original ideals. It is also plain that I am rapidly being forced to choose between Moscow and the best of my fellow Czechoslovaks. Brezhnev's 'understanding', and the criticism of *The 3,000 Words*, are both historically necessary in the situation and both dishearten me profoundly. If I were to pursue my course any further I would find myself forced into a position which, up to now, I had consistently avoided: one in which my government was caught between the demands of the Czechs and Slovaks for real democracy and those of the Russians for sham democracy. To both, I had become a touchstone, a symbol, of what might go wrong.

And yet, I am unwilling to abandon what has been achieved so far. Reform, after all, is better than repression. Democracy and human values would just have to wait. Czechoslovakia might not have a human face for a long time yet, but, at least, it could wear a face like Kadar's in Hungary.

It takes me a little time to make the arrangements—a few

weeks of discreet conversations, of reshuffling in the Praesidium, the government and the federal assembly. It is necessary to fix it first so that the man with the right qualities would have the job. But he was there, waiting. He had fought against the Nazis; he had been in prison under Novotny; he had been tortured; he was a friend of writers and poets; and he was probably the most intellectual Communist since Lenin. He was also bloody tough. When everything is ready, I announce on the night of 21 August, my resignation, and Gustav Husak is immediately elected First Secretary of the Party.

As a result, the Czechoslovak reforms survived. Husak rapidly established an agreeable relationship with the Soviet Union. He locked up the more clamorous intellectuals, but did not feel the need to torture them. Perhaps it was better than the alternative possibility: that things might have got out of hand and the Russians invaded.

I am still convinced that I did the right thing; but when I remember the Prague Spring and the passionate creation of a new human ideal in which we were all involved at the time, I wonder now what it was all about . . .

3

Well, there we are. Just as the Warsaw Letter expressed in the sharpest possible form the hysterical anxiety of phoney socialism when confronted with those human values which Dubcek came to represent, so the real *Two Thousand Words*, which was circulated in Czechoslovakia in the summer, bore the most eloquent testimony to the spirit of the Prague Spring. It was written without Dubcek's knowledge or approval, but it offered the unequivocal support of the people of Czechoslovakia for every attempt he made to stand up to Soviet pressure. Even to the point of fighting, if need be. Dubcek, in keeping with his whole approach, hoped until the very end to find a peaceful resolution to the conflict. One might say that in this sense that he did not match the expectations which were expressed in the *Two Thousand Words*. Other members of his government disagreed, but he himself, though no longer able to trust the Russians as implicitly as once he had, was still prepared to accept that *his* idea of compromise could meet *their* idea of compromise. Since it couldn't, the cheap and easy thing to say would be that Dubcek was neither canny enough to play the political game as some of his colleagues wished, nor resolute enough to fulfil the aspirations of his people.

But to say so would be to ignore the whole nature of his achievement and of what happened in Czechoslovakia in 1968. For the transformation of the country lay not so much in the actual measures promulgated by the government as in the creation of a new set of attitudes, a new kind of relationship between the governors and the governed: in short, a new spirit. Like all such transformations—which Tolstoy called migrations of the soul—it is hard to summarize after the event, or even to remember properly. But in that Spring, certain manifestations of this new spirit were clearly to be seen. The newly unshackled press, for example, did not abuse its freedom by lapsing into political irresponsibility or into cheesecake and trivia on the Western model. Instead it became a forum for serious discussions between citizen and citizen of the new society they were trying to create. Or again: hundreds of thousands of factory workers in Czechoslovakia, inoculated by many years of official propaganda against real trust in any government, were slow to respond to Dubcek's appeal. Reasonably enough, in view of their living conditions and of the fact that the country was undergoing a serious economic crisis, they wanted to know what was in it for them. Dubcek's government was indeed committed to a fundamental overhaul of the economy and a series of drastic reforms, though it never had time to formulate these properly, let alone implement them. What was clear in the first instance, though, was that the country simply could not pay its workers more. Yet instead of fobbing them off with false promises or buying their support

at the expense of a long-term programme, Dubcek and his
Economics Minister went ahead and discussed the situation
with them. They did so in public and private, in a series of
meetings, and on television. And the remarkable thing was
that this mark of trust and confidence, this ability to tell the
truth and stick to it, won them growing support. Every enquiry
that has been pieced together since that time indicates that by
the early summer Dubcek's government was as beloved in the
factories as in the homes of writers. Indeed, had it not been so,
the spontaneous resistance of the railway workers, or of the
television technicians, to the Soviet invasion could never have
happened.

It was the power of this new spirit which was fundamental
to the tranformation of Czechoslovakia—and to the motives for
the Soviet invasion. Why did Alexander Dubcek represent it
in such an extraordinary way? It is surely because, in his
person and in his mind, he carried out the redemption of a
whole people from their history. Czechoslovakia had not, in
general, shown a spirited ability to resist totalitarian onslaughts.
After the German Nazis had taken the country over (needless
to say, with British and French acquiescence), the Republic's
army produced a marching song which must be uniques
'*Gone and gone for ever*' goes the refrain—and it emphasizes
how the Germans took the lot while the Czechs and Slovaks
were unwilling to fight. Similarly, the size of the Communist
vote in the elections of 1946 indicates that many people were
simply unwilling to face the monstrous nature of Stalin's
system or the horrifying threat which loomed before those
liberties which the reborn Republic had been able to revive. But
it was because Dubcek was a product of the Stalinist system,
because he had been trained by the Comintern, because he
carried, in the course of his life, the history of Czechoslovakia,
that he was able, from the basis of his own astonishing understanding of what was at stake in 1968, to offer the people of
Czechoslovakia an opportunity to resolve their history. And in
this sense, it was he who made the *Two Thousand Words*
possible.

'There has been great alarm recently,' said the document, 'over the prospect of foreign forces interfering in our development. Whatever superior forces may face us, all we can do is stick to our positions, behave decently and start nothing ourselves. We can show our government that we will stand by it, with weapons if need be, if it will do what we give it a mandate to do.' This tone of decency, of which the only Western representative in recent years has been George Orwell, was the fundamental characteristic of that soon-to-vanish Spring. But, said the manifesto also, 'Truth is not winning the day: the truth is merely what remains when everything else has been frittered away. So there is no reason for national jubilation, simply for fresh hope.' This reason for fresh hope was provided by the man who realized that indeed everything else had been frittered away, and who, gradually, came to commit himself and his nation to decency and truth instead. It was part of the price he paid that his pilgrimage was incomplete when the Soviet Union and its allies invaded; it was his victory that, before that event, the *Two Thousand Words* had been published.

In these circumstances, is there any point in asking whether Dubcek should have been a better politician? Or whether, even, he could have averted the invasion? Probably he could have done so. Today, Czechoslovakia would no doubt be an easier place to breathe in. The degree of relative liberty which is available in one or two other Eastern European countries would also make life more enjoyable there. Husak, instead of being the faithful henchman of Soviet rule which he is, could indeed have become a semi-independent Kadar. But the spirit of the Prague Spring would never have come into existence; Czechoslovakia would stand for nothing in human consciousness.

The choice is far from easy. Who, in a comfortable Western sitting-room, would dare to tell the people of Czechoslovakia that they should have suffered less and that they should therefore have abandoned the fresh hope that they themselves had created? Dubcek was dedicated to the hope, and his people were with him. And it has not died. While the country is certainly today one of the most repressive in Eastern Europe, complete with psychiatric clinics and the rest for those who dare to challenge the official orthodoxy, it is also the home of *Charter 77*—of a demand which is growing, against all official repression, for the observance of that human decency and hope which was expressed under the short rule of Alexander Dubcek. That creation of a new human ideal was not wasted or lost; and the author of *Two Thousand Words*, Ludvik Vaculik, is also one of the people who drew up *Charter 77*. It was not 'Gone and gone for ever'. In Czechoslovakia, and in other countries of Eastern Europe, he and those who think like him, are doing the work for us all. It began in 1968.

If I had been ...

SALVADOR ALLENDE IN 1972–3

'How I would have stayed in power in Chile.'

HAROLD BLAKEMORE

1

In September 1970, in a free and democratic poll, the Chilean voters elected as president Dr Salvador Allende for a six-year term. Himself a lifelong member of the Socialist Party, Allende headed a largely-Marxist coalition of political parties, including the Communists, known as Unidad Popular (UP), a coalition which was far from united on ideology and tactics but which had come together to fight the presidential election on a common programme of sweeping social and economic change. Among the measures envisaged was the nationalization of foreign-owned mineral resources, notably copper and iron-ore; state control of private banks, domestic and foreign; rapid acceleration of land reform to break up great estates; a foreign policy which included recognition of socialist and communist states and closer relations with them, and all this while preserving traditional Chilean freedoms of political association and expression, and the independence of such bodies as the armed forces and the universities from political interference.

The rapid implementation of this programme in 1970 and 1971, however, was carried out largely without the cooperation of the Chilean legislature, the Congress, where the government had minority support: nationalization took place outside the customary legislative rules, first, by the purchase of shares to acquire control through the State Development Corporation; secondly, by the resurrection of long-forgotten but unrepealed laws of the early 1930s which empowered the executive to intervene in industries

*which were deemed to have failed in their economic functions,
and, thirdly, by such devices as strict price controls, which
reduced profit margins, and statutory higher wages to the same
effect of forcing private owners out. Outside politics, extreme
left-wing groups fomented 'direct action', seizing lands, factories,
dwellings and other privately-owned assets. The Congressional
Opposition, composed largely of the right-wing National Party
(PN) and the centrist Christian Democratic Party (PDC),
reacted strongly, and bitter political strife ensued. Politics moved
to the streets as the extreme wings of the political spectrum
adopted more violent tactics in pursuit of their objectives.*

*Efforts to achieve a dialogue between government and the
opposition PDC—the largest party in Congress—were made
throughout this period, the most serious in the middle of 1972,
but, in the event, they all foundered, against a background of
political and constitutional impasse and increasing economic
distress. The government's policy of redistributing income, which
succeeded in the short run in keeping employment high, utilizing
spare industrial capacity and increasing workers' purchasing
power, soon ran out of steam, as owners ceased to invest and
bottlenecks emerged. Higher consumption led to higher imports,
not least of foodstuffs, the internal production of which had been
disrupted by illegal land seizures, and the fall in the country's
productive capacity created balance-of-payments problems.
Nationalization of the large American copper companies without
compensation antagonized the international financial community,
whose leading member, the United States, under President Nixon,
was already committed to a policy of 'de-stabilizing' the regime
in Chile through economic pressure. Mismanagement of the
Chilean economy at both the national and local level was compounded by a fall in the world price of copper, Chile's chief export.*

*The polarization of Chilean politics and society became acute.
It was punctuated by a series of crises, such as the strike of
lorry-owners and shopkeepers in late 1972, a strike which was
only—and temporarily—suspended after the inclusion of service
officers in government, a move which produced only a short-
lived calm. Meanwhile, accelerating inflation, the growth of a*

huge black market in goods and currency, increasing social and political disorder, partly fuelled by the covert action of the CIA, all testified to the general breakdown of the Chilean economy and of Chilean society.

Finally, in September 1973, Allende's government having been declared unconstitutional by the Congressional majority and by the courts, the armed services and police took coordinated action to overthrow the government in a well-planned and swiftly-executed coup. Allende himself probably committed suicide in the presidential palace which had been strafed from the air and subjected to ground assault. The military junta, led by General Augusto Pinochet, which assumed control of Chile on September 11, 1973, systematically and ruthlessly eliminated Marxists from public life, put the other political parties into cold storage, declared its resolve to retain power until a new institutional and economic order had been created, and embarked upon an authoritarian political and economic programme involving great hardship for the mass of the people.

2

On September 18, 1982, the one hundred and seventy-second anniversary of Chile's first national government, Dr Salvador Allende, president from 1970 to 1976, was interviewed by a reporter of the well-known Chilean weekly, *Ercilla*,[1] Manuel Rodríguez. Allende, now 74 years of age, but still very active, is generally regarded as a key agent in enabling Chile, in contrast to most other South American states, to avoid military intervention in politics, pursue progressive economic and social policies within a framework of democratic party politics, and to follow a pragmatic foreign policy of amicable relations with most other countries. The interview took place at Allende's country seat, 'Unidad Popular', in the Maipó valley, some ten miles from Santiago.

RODRIGUEZ: May I begin, Don Salvador, by asking your opinion of the recent triumph of Dr Felipe Herrera in the presidential election, to succeed Don Eduardo Frei[2] after his second term of office?

ALLENDE: Well, I am, of course, delighted at this result, which is clear testimony of the continuity of the system we were able to establish in the 1970s. Felipe Herrera, as you know, is a well-known international figure, who has led the Social Democratic Alliance with distinction in opposition to Don Eduardo's party, and I have every confidence that he will enhance both his own reputation and that of the country in his coming term. I think that we shall continue to steer our traditional middle course between the competing ideologies which still divide the major nations of the world.

RODRIGUEZ: Yes, I agree with your estimate. But the remarkable internal progress we have made in the past ten years, and our high international reputation, were not inevitable, were they? I am thinking of the early years of your own presidency when it was really touch and go with our long democratic tradition. Could we begin by going back to your own election in September 1970? What were your own feelings that night when you had won. though very narrowly?

ALLENDE: 'Narrowly' is not too strong a word! By some 39,000 votes in an electorate of about three-and-a-half million! And, of course, the opposition parties were in a majority in Congress. But, on that night, my feelings were, very mixed. I was elated, and frankly somewhat surprised, at the thought that I had won the presidency at the fourth attempt, and after nearly forty years of political activity. On the other hand, although the Popular Unity alliance had come together to fight the election, it was far from united on either means or objectives.

Then, again, many of our supporters never expected us to win, and, in fact, we ourselves were hardly prepared for government. We had published our programme, of course, but putting it into effect was clearly going to be difficult.

RODRIGUEZ: Before you go on, Don Salvador, would you say a little more about the Popular Unity Alliance, because in your first two years it did, indeed, seem at times that it would break up?

ALLENDE: Well, I said 'alliance', though 'coalition' would be a better description. Apart from the bigger parties, the Socialist, Communist and Radical, there were three further, smaller groupings, including the Movement of Unitary Popular Action (MAPU), which had hived off from the PDC, believing it was not radical enough. My own Socialist Party was sharply divided, as it had long been, between what you might call the 'moderates' and the 'revolutionaries'. I had always believed myself in a 'Chilean road to socialism', that is, a programme of sweeping change but one which would be carried out constitutionally, preserving our party political democracy, free speech, the right of free association, and so on.

Many of my closest colleagues shared this view. But the more revolutionary wing, personified really by Carlos Altamirano,[3] did not agree. They had much more in common with the ultra left-wing groups outside politics, the Movement of the Revolutionary Left (MIR), the Organized Vanguard of the People (VOP) and so on, in holding that the power we had got through elections should be used violently and ruthlessly to destroy the existing system, and put something altogether different in its place. I remember many fierce arguments with my own nephew, Pascal, on the very subject—he belonged to the MIR. Well, he and Altamirano and many others really thought that, once in power, we could so mobilize the masses as to change the institutional structure of Chile radically almost overnight. They based this view on their interpretation of Chilean society which took class as the touchstone. Of course, class-divisions were acute, but I thought their view a bit simplistic, since who could say what the 'bourgeoisie' in Chile was, when there were so many small property-holders and tiny businesses that could certainly not be lumped with the real aristocrats, yet who, in the eyes of my very left-wing friends, ought to disappear as 'class-enemies' of the proletariat? Such beliefs did immense harm in my first two years and almost wrecked everything.

RODRIGUEZ: And what about the Communists?

ALLENDE: The Communists, led by Secretary-General Luis Corvalán[4] were, perhaps paradoxically, with us in believing that, in Chile, you had to make your revolution by carrying the people with you, and this meant making haste slowly—Fabianism, I believe the British Labour Party calls it—and not antagonizing the uncommitted by putting the fear of death into them. He had the best-disciplined party in our system then and a much more realistic view of our history and society than did Alta-mirano and the *miristas*. He was consistently cautious, wanted to maintain a broad alliance, including even the left-wing of the PDC, led by Radomiro Tomic,[5] who, after his defeat in 1970, was certainly prepared to give us a fair chance. Oh, yes, the Communists were certainly far less 'revolutionary' than many Socialists, though whether this was purely tactical is anybody's guess.

RODRIGUEZ: And the Radicals?

ALLENDE: Well, the Radicals were in a difficult position for a party which had dominated government in the 1940s and much of the 1950s. Having lost the middle ground to the Christian Democrats in the 1960s, they had no political future there, or with the Right, so they threw in their lot with us, even at the cost of splitting the party. A year after my election, they even formally went Marxist! But, then, they were a pretty opportunist lot, the politicians, I mean.

RODRIGUEZ: What about the post-election period? If I remember rightly, the two months between your election in September and your actual take-over of the presidency in November were a time of great perturbation, and I think you yourself would now admit making a number of mistakes.

ALLENDE: Well, you must remember that we were a minority government with the opposition parties in control of Congress, and yet our supporters, ebullient over this long-awaited electoral triumph, naturally expected rapid action. At the same time, it was clear that the wild men of the Right, and with the support of some foreign economic elements, would stop at nothing. The election saw a panic run on the banks, in Congress the National Party tried to block the popular will by getting Alessandri[6] declared the winner, and, then, of course, there was the brutal assassination of General René Schneider, C-in-C of the army and a firm believer in the non-intervention of the military in politics. His assassins bungled a kidnap attempt, hoping to get him to stop what they though was revolution through the ballot box and, since the PDC refused all along to support the Congressional plot, and Schneider's death shocked the country, my election was ratified by the legislature according to constitutional practice and long-standing precedent.[7] I had to accept a PDC document guaranteeing long-standing freedoms, but I was happy to do that since I believed in them myself.

I did, however, make one misjudgement arising out of the Schneider affair. I let my more militant colleagues persuade me that his murder was an act of strength by the extreme Right, when, in reality, it was an act of weakness, and agreed to have a personal bodyguard, the *Grupo de Amigos del Presidente* (GAP), plain-clothes armed men, some of whom, I'm afraid, had rather dubious backgrounds. At the same time, since it was customary for a new president to perform some act of clemency, I yielded to similar pressures in offering amnesty to a number of extreme leftists who were awaiting trial for violent acts, including my own nephew and a lot of his pals. These two things certainly upset a lot of people. Chileans are very conscious of tradition, and many didn't like what I had done. But, don't forget it was an uncertain time, and that there were plenty of extremists about, Left as well as Right, who were quite capable of violence, as events were to reveal.

RODRIGUEZ: Your election programme, the Basic Programme of Popular Unity, was pretty sweeping, though, wasn't it? I mean, it must have alarmed a lot of people with its talk of widespread nationalization, expropriation of foreigners, new relations with Marxist states, and so on?

ALLENDE: Of course it was! But, you see, we didn't come into power to sit on our backsides. There were—there still are—deep social and economic problems affecting Chile and its people. We wanted to narrow class-divisions in Chile, to do away with a system of land tenure which, despite Frei's efforts, still left the landless and very poor as the vast majority, to diversify our economy away from critical dependence on copper, and recover the ownership of our natural resources from foreigners. We wanted to end malnutrition and eliminate slums, to educate all our children and give them jobs when they grew up, and provide people with decent housing. And to do some things, we felt it necessary to give the state a much bigger role in running the economy and society. The big problem was how to do these things without a Congressional majority, to keep up the momentum from 1970, satisfy our supporters and, indeed, gain a lot more.

We had endless debates within the UP about our strategy and tactics, and I can tell you it was a hell of a job to get agreement. ALL the parties insisted on sharing our ministerial posts on a kind of *pro rata* basis: if Minister X were to be a Communist, then Deputy Minister Y had to be a Socialist, and Sub-Minister Z, a Radical, irrespective of actual competence. It was crazy, but I had to go along with it for long enough since, for all the rhetoric of reform and even revolution, a lot of our leading figures were simply after jobs. Time and time again, I asked for a free hand in filling posts, but didn't get it, and our unity then was too fragile for me to insist.

RODRIGUEZ: Can you tell me something about the political tactics your government decided to adopt?

ALLENDE: Well, that question caused endless discussion, too! Should we behave like a 'normal' elected Chilean government, put bills into Congress to be passed into law, when we were in a minority there? It is true that the PDC were divided between, broadly, Frei's following, who thought we wanted to create a one-party state, and those around Tomic who wanted to give us a fair wind, but the usual procedure seemed a risky course, putting bills in only to get them held up in debate, watered down or thrown out altogether. I hadn't spent nearly

forty years in Congress without seeing its capacity
for obstruction and prevarication, and, frankly, I'd
done quite a bit of that myself as President of the
Senate in Frei's first period.

Take the issue of nationalizing the banks. The
Communists thought the *tomicistas* would probably back that in Congress and wanted to do a deal
with them, whereas chaps on our side like Altamirano were all for direct action, mobilizing bank
clerks to seize premises, stop work, and so force
the business through. This was madness, of course,
though it was precisely what the MIR were doing
on the land, inciting peasants to seize farms, and
that led owners to kill off livestock or drive it
through the *cordillera* to Argentina, so we had to
spend more on importing food, with disastrous
effects on our balance of payments.

But to come back to the banks. We finally hit on
the idea of using the Development Corporation
(CORFO) to buy out private stock-holders at a
certain price, with more than a nod that the longer
they delayed selling, the more the price would fall.
On other enterprises, Eduardo Novoa[8] came up
with a brilliant idea. He found that an old law,
passed way back in the early 1930s in the short-
lived, so-called Socialist Republic, had never been
repealed. It was a vaguely-worded law, empowering
the state to take over suppliers who were deemed
to have failed the people, so we resurrected it and
used it extensively to intervene in all kinds of
businesses.

We thought at the time we were being pretty
clever, especially since neither of these acts was
strictly unconstitutional, given the immense powers
our system confers on the president. But they were
examples of changing the rules while the game is
being played, and the Congressional opposition

really got upset as their function was by-passed. Still, this was a heady period, when we even turned a blind eye to all kinds of illegalities going on—land and factory seizures, sit-ins, and so on. In fact, a lot of our officials actually told the *cara-bineros* that they were not to interfere, and this naturally riled that elite force whose whole training was based on respect for law and order.

Another area where we probably went too far early on was in allowing Chile to become a second kind of Cuba, taking in people who called themselves political exiles from elsewhere in Latin America without much immigration control. Naturally, the fact of being the first state in the world freely to elect a Marxist at its head attracted a lot of international interest from people all over the place—English doctors, French intellectuals, socialist members of Parliament from Western Europe. A lot were just curious, some sought a solution to personal problems by serving our revolution, but the 'political exiles' became a tremendous liability. They hitched up with the MIR, got involved in all sorts of clandestine activities, and were a key factor in the increasing polarization of opinion within the country. The extremist Right really made hay with the situation all these developments were creating. Not that they wouldn't have opposed us anyway, but they gained more credibility among the uncommitted whose support we needed.

RODRIGUEZ: That certainly is true. I remember myself how worried I was at the way things were going and what the government was doing. For example, the visit of Fidel Castro to Chile in the latter part of 1971 seemed to me to be a deliberate provocation.

ALLENDE: I can see that, and, in fact, I think the visit helped him more than me, in breaking down the hemispheric isolation of Cuba—still pretty solid at the time, and it brought us very few benefits. His rather exotic though, in some ways, endearing approach did not chime in with Chilean styles of public behaviour, and his public support of my view—that each country makes its own revolution best by conformity with its history and tradition— did not please the MIR or many Socialists, who wanted more revolutionary rhetoric from one of their great heroes. But I had to demonstrate our freedom of action in foreign policy and that Chile sought good relations with all countries, irrespective of ideology. And you have to remember that, at that time, pressure from the United States was already building up. It was only four months after Fidel's visit in November 1971, that the ITT case[10] came to light, though the revelation of the real degree to which the Nixon administration was prepared to go to oppose us only came out after the notorious Watergate affair and Nixon's resignation.[11] Their own 'credit squeeze' and influence in international financial organizations made things very tough for us at times.

RODRIGUEZ: Was it crucial?

ALLENDE: That is a difficult one. It depends on one's analysis of the impact of our first year and a half, say to about March 1971. We started in 1970 with a deliberate policy of raising wages and controlling prices in order to redistribute income to benefit the poor, and benefit they certainly did. Their new, higher consumption pattern—long overdue in our view—had a most beneficial, immediate effect on the consumer-goods industries which were able to utilize spare capacity and keep employment high.

These economic policies which, to be frank, had clear political objectives, paid off handsomely in the short run. In the municipal elections of

April 1971, we got over fifty per cent of the vote, though we did not do so well in by-elections for Congressional seats in January 1972, by which time our economic problems had increased, and for the following reasons. The redistributive policy of Economy Minister, Pedro Vuscovic, which we all accepted, did raise the standard of living of the poor considerably, and it also consolidated and broadened our political base. But it also hammered private enterprise, and we still had a mixed economy. Pricing policies, exchange regulations, nationalization and increasing control over imports created a complete lack of confidence among private investors and owners, so the boom soon petered out and it was not long before actual disinvestment started.

Similarly on the land, agrarian reform had been speeded up by Minister of Agriculture Jacques Chonchol, while the MIR complicated the process by fomenting peasant seizures of land and rural assets. Landowners simply packed up, investment stopped, production slumped precisely at the time when people with more money in their pockets than ever before were eating well, often for the first time in their lives. We just had to import more food to meet the demand, our reserves fell alarmingly and, simultaneously, the world market price of our major export, copper, was falling alarmingly—from about £750 a ton in April 1970, to about £420 a ton in January 1971, less than the price on which we had based our budget calculations. And nationalization had dislocated our own output. Finally, in 1972 we were due to repay some $300m of our colossal foreign debt, so we had no alternative to seeking re-scheduling and increasing prices at home. The gilt was off the gingerbread. So, to come back to your original question, I would have to say that, though economic pressure from the United States compounded our problems, it did not create them.

RODRIGUEZ: So, what you are saying is that it was the economic situation in 1971 and 1972 which really determined political events?

ALLENDE: Yes, indeed. Of course, as a good Marxist myself, I had always believed that in order to change society and politics in Chile, we needed to transform the economic structure. But the sweeping changes we had already made and, perhaps more importantly, the *way* we had made them, were not only anathema to the Right but also, and increasingly, to the middle ground of Chilean politics, and it is there that compromise takes place. In other words, the sheer pace of change, our unorthodox style and, above all, the tactics of direct action pursued by the ultra-Left, were alienating people whose support we really needed. The 'Chilean road to socialism' was taking the wrong direction.

RODRIGUEZ: Could you elaborate on this?

ALLENDE: I would put it this way. When I said 'the Chilean road to socialism,' the emphasis was on the adjective. For a programme of radical change but without violence, we had tremendous advantages no other Latin American state possessed. Take the Marxist parties and the trade unions, for example. Now, where else in this continent have these bodies been so integrated into the democratic political process as here? Or, take the armed forces: where else in Latin America have they got the esteem they have in Chile for strict adherence to professional duties and avoidance of political intervention? It is in our nature, in our historical experience, to encourage the tolerance of conflicting views in politics, to seek for compromise between antagonistic philosophies in looking for a better life for our people.

Until 1970, despite immense strains in our social fabric, and despite certain breakdowns which were probably inevitable, as in the early 1930s, we had managed to move to a system of accommodation in politics, of gradual change, though at an accelerating pace. In fact, despite its failures to complete its programme, Frei's government which preceded mine performed one huge historic task— it made fundamental change broadly acceptable right across the political spectrum, and, to most Chileans, my election was an indication of continuity, not of violent revolution. Only the extremes, on Right and Left, did not share this view, the Right seeking to perpetuate a system of class domination long since doomed, the Left taking the politics of hatred as its guide, and that was singularly unconstructive.

RODRIGUEZ: But, surely, in your first two years, as you yourself have just hinted, the government itself had shattered the political equilibrium?

ALLENDE: I would say seriously strained, rather than shattered. I was, after all, only human. Here I was on that September night in 1970, the man who had attained supreme office, having been denied it three times before, surrounded by different groups, each with its own formula for the future, and faced by a heterogeneous but powerful opposition. Nor could I be unaffected by the popular response to my electoral triumph—the torchlight processions, the faces of the masses who saw in my election the dawn of an unimagined day, the flying banners and the chanted slogans. It was a euphoric time. Moreover, the opposition was then demoralized by defeat, despite its Congressional majority, and it was deeply divided. The National Party would oppose us, but it was not large. The Christian

Democrats, far more numerous, were deeply split,
as I mentioned earlier. As long as the opposition
was so divided, our Congressional minority didn't
matter much, especially as we were by-passing
Congress anyway. But, as the economic situation
deteriorated, as the extreme right-wing organizations, such as *Patria y Libertad* (Fatherland and
Freedom) and the extreme Left, such as the MIR,
took politics on to the streets, and law and order
began to break down, the opposition were encouraged to make common cause, paradoxically
just as the debate about tactics in our own ranks
grew more embittered.

By then—early 1972—our economy really was
breaking down; our political life had become
polarized, and the armed forces and police, despite
the firm stand of army C-in-C, General Carlos
Prats, that their constitutional duty was to support
the government, come what may, were appalled at
the deterioration in public life. Some in the high
commands, in fact, were already talking about the
necessity to intervene. By then, indeed, and in
contrast to my feelings on election night, I felt
more alone than Crusoe on his island, but also
quite convinced that we had reached a critical
juncture and needed to reappraise both our policies
and methods.

RODRIGUEZ: Did this conviction grow on you gradually or was
it brought home by particular events?

ALLENDE: A mixture of the two. As the situation deteriorated,
particularly from mid-1971, I few increasingly
despondent at the way things were going, but
specific events that year also catalyzed my impressions. First, in June, Edmundo Pérez Zujovic,
Frei's former Minister of the Interior, was murdered by members of the VOP, which had
benefited from my political amnesty; then, in

August, 500 supervisors at the Chuquicamata copper-mine—recently nationalized—went on strike in protest at political appointments there; third, our plan to nationalize the company producing the nation's newsprint—it was, after all, virtually a monopoly—raised fears of state control of the press, and finally, in December 1971, there was a march of upper- and middle-class housewives with empty pans, protesting at food shortages, which was broken up by militant youths on our side. I was much more shocked by the murder of Pérez than by the march of the housewives, but all these events were evidence of the deteriorating situation which was uniting the opposition in Congress and providing fuel for our external enemies.

In January 1972, came clear evidence of electoral disfavour when we lost—and heavily—by-elections for Congressional seats in O'Higgins and Colchagua, and in Linares. These were regions with large agricultural population, and O'Higgins contains the big copper-mining complex of El Teniente, so, in view of what we had done for the workers, we naturally expected to win. Our defeat, however, stirred up the most bitter dispute in our ranks, the Communists blaming the MIR, and Altamirano arguing that only direct action would consolidate the revolution. The elation of the opposition was then increased a month later when we simply had to put up prices, raising the cost of living by no less than 13 %.

Things were falling apart. By now, the economy really was in a mess. Inflation from January to June 1972, was over 27 %, more than twice the rate for the same period in 1971; we had a deficit of over $300m in our balance of payments for 1971; exports were falling, imports, especially of food, rising, and we had had to increase the note issue by 173 % in 1971. The black market in food and foreign currency was now huge, and the sharp conjunction of an economic crisis and political confrontation, including frequent street battles, was obvious to anyone with eyes to see it.

RODRIGUEZ: What, then, did you decide to do? Presumably, any move that you might make towards the opposition was bound to split your own ranks while, at the same time, letting things go on as they were was probably even more dangerous?

ALLENDE: You're dead right! On the one hand, by mid-1972, direct action had got a lot of people involved—peasants, workers, and so on—and the disastrous economic effects were of secondary consequence to the political significance of land and factory seizures for those who instigated them. They wanted to politicize the masses, and put pressure on us, and they did pretty well. After all, it's very exciting for a worker, long accustomed to defer to the boss, suddenly to be told that the factory belongs to him and his *compañeros*! To clamp down on such activities would certainly create enormous difficulties within the UP. But, on the other hand, to get a more conciliatory mood from the opposition by such action on my part would have been putting my head in the lion's mouth, since, having demoralized my own support, I might find them exacting a price I could not pay.

This was the big question: had we already gone too far in deserting our traditional system of compromise to try to return to it without complete disaster? I spent many sleepless nights in mid-1972 pondering that question. I had to keep the great gains we had made but still hope to secure the support of enough of the middle ground to isolate and nullify the extremists.

RODRIGUEZ: Were there any factors at all in your favour in seeking to do this?

ALLENDE: Yes, there were. First, we could rely on the Church under the Cardinal Archbishop of Santiago, Raúl Silva: he had been consistently in favour of peaceful reform, and his influence, particularly with our womenfolk, was one moderate force we might tap. Then, there were the services. While some higher officers were more anti-politics altogether than a-political, the majority agreed with the late René Schneider and with Carlos Prats that their duty was to support responsible government. They could help to cool the temperature, provided we could do more than simply condemn verbally all the illegal and violent acts that were going on: this is what was eroding their habits of obedience to the civil power, all these armed groups going around challenged their corporate nature as *the* guardians of the state.

Then, there still remained some hope of an understanding with the Christian Democrat opposition and with smaller groups like the Independent Radicals. Neither was happy with their coalition with the National Party, and would have liked to be a 'loyal opposition', but they felt they had been pushed into confrontation with a government that gave them no alternative. On the economic side, perhaps we could make some constructive gestures towards foreign investors and domestic capitalists which would restore confidence and, finally, I had myself to act more like the President of the Republic and less like the leader of an ill-fitting political coalition than I had done so far.

RODRIGUEZ: What, then, were your first steps in this new direction?

ALLENDE: Taking advantage of a serious incident in May 1972, when Communists and the MIR clashed in

Concepción, with one killed and forty injured, I
abandoned my role of impartial chairman in the
subsequent fierce debate in the governing coalition
and came down heavily on the Communist side.
Corvalán argued for public condemnation of
illegal seizures, an all-out attack on right-wing
extremists, a new dialogue with the PDC, an end
to distribution of government posts on party lines,
and a planned economic policy to combat inflation and increase production. I backed him all
the way. I then rang the Cardinal and asked him
to act as go-between with the PDC, and drafted a
memo for discussions with them. I also arranged a
nationwide TV and radio broadcast to explain the
situation, announcing what I had done and not
mincing any words about the gravity of the political
and economic state of the nation. At the same
time, I sent for the heads of the services and the
police force, reminding them that I was not only
President, but also Commander-in-Chief of the
services, and asking for full cooperation in curbing
extremism on both wings.

RODRIGUEZ: I imagine the ultra-Left was furious? What
happened then?

ALLENDE: Of course they were: Altamirano and the MIR
accused me of selling out to the bourgeoisie,
betraying the revolution, and God knows what!
They threatened to mobilize the workers and
peasants, organize huge demonstrations, speed up
takeovers and positively seek confrontation, not
only with the obvious opposition forces but also
with the government. But here I had a couple of
aces to play. The first—which I hoped myself
would be largely bluff—was to threaten to call in
the forces to dispossess illegal occupants of
factories and so on; and secondly, I decided to go
on a series of walkabouts of factories, explaining

the situation face-to-face with the workers. Well, as you know, the presidency has immense prestige if it is used in the right way, and I really found myself enjoying that role of someone who, though the leader of a particular political coalition, was somehow above politics as father of the nation. Another thing I had to do to carry this off was to dissolve the GAP, against a lot of opposition from personal friends who thought I was mad to do this, in view of the threats from the extreme Right. But I thought it a risk worth taking in the circumstances, and it certainly helped to foster a better atmosphere.

RODRIGUEZ: But how did the Christian Democrats react to this apparent volte-face? It must have been difficult in view of the polemic between you, not to mention the vicious personal attacks on Frei by your partisans.

ALLENDE: This was my greatest worry, that they might suspect the olive branch as a trick. Fortunately, they did respond positively, thanks not least to their president, Renán Fuentealba, who was very cooperative in getting talks going and managed to persuade the Party as a whole at least to explore possibilities of accommodation with us. Of course, the National Party was livid, but that didn't matter, since it was in our mutual interests to isolate both extremes. The PDC responded partly because their enforced coalition with the National Party was a marriage of convenience with a group which had opposed all their own reforms in government and, secondly, they knew that it was imperative if they were going to defeat us and keep our system intact that they do so through the ballot box, and the feeling of violence went right against their philosophy and conduct. It was in both our interests to stop matters short of the point where

Chileans lost all faith in traditional methods. So,
by July 1972, we had at least got a dialogue going.
RODRIGUEZ: Of what did it consist?
ALLENDE: Well, you will recollect our initial policy of large-
scale nationalization. The PDC had long wanted
a strict definition of which areas of the economy
should pass to the state, which should remain in
private hands, and which should be mixed state
and private enterprise. They had a bill in Congress
since October 1971, to define these areas and to
insist that all future nationalizations should be
subject to Congressional approval. We, of course,
had a minority there, but I, as president, had a
constitutional veto over legislation which could
only be overridden by a two-thirds vote of both
Houses sitting together, and the opposition were
short of that number. This issue had given rise to
fierce arguments, the opposition as a whole
claiming that a simple majority vote, rather than
two-thirds, was enough to override the presidential
veto, while we simply carried on with our 'back-
door' take-overs through 'intervention' and so on.
If we could agree with the PDC some formula for
resolving this constitutional deadlock, we would
be well on the way to a better understanding.

It took a fortnight of tough bargaining to reach
understanding with the PDC on this. They finally
agreed to let certain nationalizations stand—
minerals, the banks, monopoly distributors and
suppliers, and we agreed that on pending cases,
such as four Chilean banks which had not yet
been taken over, we would implement long-
cherished plans of theirs for a system of workers'
control, the details to be worked out by a joint
commission. We also withdrew our plans to
nationalize newsprint. On land reform, it was
agreed that take-overs under Frei's Agrarian

Reform Act would stand, and another mixed commission would validate illegal seizures or reject them. On the difficult question of factory seizures, many of which, frankly, were in a mess owing to the lack of trained managers and accountants, it was decided to implement a scheme of co-partnership with workers' councils, joint worker-manager committees, with both workers and owners participating in profits. Politically, we both agreed to crack down on both the extreme Right and the extreme Left, to moderate our propaganda against one another and, without surrendering our rights to act as responsible government and opposition respectively, to cooperate in Congressional committees to speed up legislation long delayed, such as the bill to benefit the Mapuche Indians which had been bogged down for two years.

RODRIGUEZ: The way you put it sounds very neat, but I suppose, in practice, this accord took some time to work out and, in effect, you both had a lot of internal opposition?

ALLENDE: You can say that again! On the PDC side, Fuentealba had a devil of a job to persuade his party that we were serious. The left wing, under Tomic, soon came round, but it was only when Frei threw his considerable and eloquent weight into the argument that the centre and right of the party agreed to explore the package, and then only subject to reappraisal after six months. Our side was much more difficult. I knew I could count on the Communists and Radicals and about half of my own Socialist party: the problem was Altamirano's following among the Socialists, the MAPU and, of course, the MIR and other revolutionary groups outside politics. On the newsprint issue, for example, I was accused of leaving this bastion of capitalist control in the hands of the bourgeoisie, but I was able to point out that its guiding hand, Jorge Alessandri, who had fought me for the presidency in 1970, had never denied supplies to the Marxist press. The biggest problem was the militant groups, many armed, behind the land and factory seizures, who seemed determined to resist any attempt to dislodge them. I had to think this one out very carefully. Finally, I had to bring in the military and the *carabineros*, but in a particular way. Now, the idea had occurred to me earlier to invite service chiefs to accept ministerial posts, in order to calm the atmosphere and persuade the opposition that we really meant what we said in attacking extremism. But, on reflection, I rejected this ploy. First, it would have upset my Communist partners, whose disciplined support I needed in the battle with the extremists, and, more importantly, it would have compromised the services themselves. For how could the constitutionally a-political military, with their strict institutional loyalty and professionalism, enter a cabinet to carry out policies which were themselves political? No, their involvement had to be achieved another way.

RODRIGUEZ: So, what did you do?

ALLENDE: Having consulted my own loyal adherents and the PDC, I called in the service chiefs again, and, with a lot of publicity, told them of the accord and asked for full cooperation in implementing it. I assured them of full presidential and Congressional backing for putting down extremism on all sides, and sent a bill to Congress, authorizing wide powers of search and investigation for arms and other evidence of unconstitutional activity. A declaration of support, drafted by Prats and unanimously approved by the other commanders, was then published and broadcast, and it had a dramatic effect.

RODRIGUEZ: But there were some disturbances, weren't there? I seem to remember a particular incident in Concepción, the *mirista* stronghold, in August 1972.

ALLENDE: Inevitably, I'm afraid. And not only in Concepción, though that was the worst case. We had a number of confrontations throughout the republic, though a lot less than one might have feared, and some people got killed and more were injured. The *carabineros*, however, now with a clear mandate, moved in quickly, arrested the ring-leaders, confiscated arms, and restored order. In fact, with the full weight of the services, the Church and the new middle ground of politics behind us, we were able to stabilize the situation. Of course, it was a lengthy process, and I haven't time to go into details. But the atmosphere had improved enormously by the end of 1972 and this contributed a good deal to improving the economic situation.

RODRIGUEZ: Yes, I was going to ask about that. After all, given the fact that economic measures take a long time to work through and our situation in mid-1972 was pretty desperate, how did it change?

ALLENDE: Well, only slowly and painfully, of course. But the new consolidation policy did create fresh confidence in our economic management, internally and externally. The real problem was copper. Now, when we nationalized the large American concerns in 1971, the big debate had been on compensation, for even the National Party had been in favour of the take-over. We were then in full flood on our programme, and I had gone so far as to say that, not only did we owe the companies nothing, but that in fact they owed us for excessive profits taken out previously! This rhetorical nationalism reflected the euphoric mood of the moment, but it did us immense harm. Now, with a changing internal set-up, I thought it right to try to repair the situation. Through the American Ambassador in Santiago, I opened negotiations with Kennecott and Anaconda[12] to settle this problem. This certainly halted the harassment of our copper exports in foreign markets which Kennecott planned to start, and, while final agreement took a long time, we eventually reached it in 1973. Meanwhile, the international 'credit squeeze' was gradually relaxed and foreign loans and credits began to flow back into Chile, though under less liberal terms than before I assumed office.

Naturally, we also had to introduce austerity measures and improve efficiency and this was pretty tough after two years of expansion. It needed a massive propaganda and educational campaign, persuading the people of the need to reduce the money supply, allowing some prices to rise, improving our tax system, and gradually replacing political interventors in factories by people who knew how to read an account book. Here, the Communist Party, with its disciplined cadres, did a first-class job, though whether Corvalán simply saw the new policy as a tactical manoeuvre rather than a basic change, I shall never know. It was the end of 1973 before we really turned the corner, but by then we had diversified our exports, improved the tax system enormously, restored some incentive to private enterprise, properly organized the rural sector, and so on. We also benefited from a rise in copper prices in 1973.

RODRIGUEZ: 1973 saw the Congressional elections, did it not? What happened then?

ALLENDE: By then, the political spectrum had shaken down

a good deal. With the curbing of the extremists, Left and Right, and with a constructive dialogue between the government and the responsible opposition, the electorate moved to the middle. The UP coalition had broken up, the Altamirano Socialists breaking away to form what they called the Authentic Socialist Party, and the MAPU reduced to a fringe party. The National Party, with 20 % of the vote, remained the bastion of private enterprise, while the PDC was now the effective alternative government to the UP coalition of, basically, my Socialists, the Communists and the Radicals. With the development of Eurocommunism in the mid-1970s, and other international currents of political change, we dropped the label of Popular Unity, as you know, in 1978, and adopted the name of the Chilean Social Democratic alliance.

RODRIGUEZ: Don Salvador, as you know, many of your former colleagues accuse you of betraying the revolutionary cause by what you did in 1972. How do you reply to your critics?

ALLENDE: Well, they only have to look at the facts. Here we are in 1982, the only welfare state in Latin America, with the commanding heights of the economy controlled by the state but still with enough room for private enterprise to operate. We produce enough food from our reformed agrarian sector to feed our people—and what other socialist state has yet managed to do that? We have diversified our economy, enjoy excellent economic relations not only with our neighbours in the Andean Pact but with capitalist and communist countries alike. Socially, much remains to be done, and always will so long as our population increases at its present rate, but the bitter class divisions of the early 1970s are much diminished, and our institutions of co-partnership in industry are the envy of the world.

Of course, the original programme of the UP of 1970 was modified, but it was modified because, as it stood, it did not conform to our history and traditions, particularly the way it was being carried out. The 'Chilean road to socialism', as I defined it, has prevailed, and the second PDC administration, just ended, has not rolled back any of the gains we made.

If we had not changed tactics in 1972, my guess is that there would have been a strong right-wing backlash in the election of 1976, assuming we could have muddled through to that date. But that is a big assumption. And, honestly, I don't think we could have done that. By mid-1972, the slide into social, political and economic anarchy was well under way, and intransigence on both sides would only have increased. Who is to say what then might have happened? We could have had either military intervention or civil war. Either would have been disastrous to our free institutions, our free press, our freedom of thought. The politics of hatred would have been institutionalized by whichever side had won, and our distinctive nature, our *Chilenidad*, would have been destroyed completely or, at least, seriously impaired. So I say to my critics, what were the alternatives at the time, and where would they have led us? It is a rhetorical question in view of what actually happened, but it is one my armchair critics might profitably ask themselves.

RODRIGUEZ: Don Salvador, thank you very much for your patience and courtesy. I'm sure our readers will enjoy these fascinating reminiscences.

ALLENDE: Thank *you* very much. And I see we have finished in good time for me to keep my next appointment,

with retired General Augusto Pinochet, who is
coming to tea. You know, he was most helpful,
as Commander of the Santiago garrison in 1973,
in putting down the very last illegal attempt, by a
small body of disaffected troops, to overthrow the
constitutional order in June. But that is another
story.

3

The history of Chile during the Allende period still arouses
passionate debate and from it are drawn the most diverse
political messages. In France and Italy, for example, you will
hear people on the radical left wing of the spectrum arguing that
the Allende experiment proved that no Marxist government
was ever going to be permitted to retain power gained as a result
of the ballot box and that the only road to power was revolution.
On the Right, plenty of analysts will be happy to tell you that
the severe economic problems that Chile was facing by mid-1972
resulted directly from the Marxist orientation of the Allende
government and that the only parties that can run an economy
(and, by implication, a political system) successfully are those
dedicated to capitalism.

   In addition to people with an overt political axe to grind,
serious historians, too, remain widely divided over their interpretation of the Allende years, and not all experts will be happy
with the argument, set out in the preceding pages, that Allende
could have reached accommodation with the Christian Democrats and thus saved his government and his skin. Many on the
Left will argue that the intransigence of the Right, in which they
include the PDC, and the unremitting hostility of the Nixon
administration, made an outcome such as is suggested here quite
impossible. Similarly, many analysts on the Right, including
some whose sympathies lie with the PDC, would argue that it

flies in the face of reason to suppose that Allende, himself a Marxist, could have moved in the direction indicated, and, indeed, that if he had done so, the reaction from his own ranks would have been more violent than is here imagined. Yet in my view, the *possibility* of accommodation between the UP government and the PDC in opposition did remain open up to the middle of 1972. In July of that year, long and serious negotiations between the two sides did take place and, it was reported at the time, they reached agreement on some 85 % of the agenda. They could surely have solved the remaining 15 % of their problems.

Allende would certainly have been predisposed to try—if we are to believe that he meant what he said in his speeches and writings where he argued again and again that the 'Chilean road to socialism' implied a high degree of continuity of the existing system as well as radical change. Even Corvalán's Communist Party, which feared the alienation of large sectors of public opinion which they sought to persuade, would have had some sympathy with Allende's efforts to rid his beleaguered UP government of the stigma of the MIR and other violent ultra-leftists.

In reality, of course, the UP-PDC talks broke down and Chile was set on a collision course. But if, as I believe, the essence of history is choice of action, the *possibility* of avoiding what actually occurred was certainly there at that time. It would have required bold and resolute decisions on both sides, with some unpleasant consequences for each, and Allende would have had to act like a statesman, rather than the clever politician he undoubtedly was. Perhaps he never could; perhaps the opposition had already made up its mind that it could do nothing but oppose; and perhaps the possibility suggested here is no more than a pipe-dream. For millions of Chileans, however, and for the international community at large, the real denouement was a total tragedy, and if we are to learn from it we should seriously ask ourselves how far it was inevitable.

NOTES

The author wishes to acknowledge with thanks helpful comments on an earlier draft by Dr Simon Collier, Professor Frederick Nunn and Torcuato S. di Tella.

1 *Ercilla* is the best-known weekly Chilean magazine of current events, somewhat similar to *Time* in its format and content.

2 Eduardo Frei Montalva (b. 1911), a leading member of the Chilean Christian Democratic Party throughout its history, led the first Christian Democratic administration in Latin America as President of Chile, 1964–70.

3 Carlos Altamirano (b. 1923), lawyer, university professor, and socialist politician. In 1971, became Secretary-General of the Socialist Party.

4 Luis Corvalán (b. 1916), lifelong Communist, Secretary-General of the party from 1957.

5 Radomiro Tomic (b. 1914), leading Christian Democrat and the party's defeated candidate in the presidential election of 1970.

6 Jorge Alessandri (b. 1896), son of President Arturo Alessandri (1920–25, 1932-38), and himself President, 1958–64. Narrowly defeated by Allende in three-cornered presidential election of 1970.

7 Under the Chilean Constitution, when a presidential candidate does not have a clear plurality over all others while receiving most votes, Congress must declare his election valid. This was the case with Allende.

8 Eduardo Novoa (b. 1916), a well-known lawyer, commissioned by the government to study the question of executive power outside the control or approval of Congress.

9 The 100-day regime of Carlos Dávila in 1932, a period of considerable unrest in Chile, following the impact of the Great Crash (1929–31) which wrecked the economy.

10 In March 1972, New York columnist Jack Anderson revealed that top men in the International Telephone and Telegraph Corporation, which had large assets in Chile, had sought government backing to create economic chaos in Chile after Allende was elected, in the hope of forcing the Chilean military to intervene.

11 After the Watergate affair, investigations by Congressional committees in the United States indicated sizable CIA activity in Chile, which had the support of the US government, against Allende.

12 Kennecott and Anaconda were the two major multinational, US-based, copper firms affected by the nationalization of Chilean copper.

NOTES ON THE CONTRIBUTORS

DANIEL SNOWMAN was born in London in 1938. After a double first in History at Cambridge and a spell studying American Government at Cornell University, he became at 24 a lecturer in Politics and American Studies at the new University of Sussex, where he remained for 4 years. Since 1967 he has been a producer of talks and documentaries with the BBC.

He has maintained his special interest in the USA, a country that he has visited and worked in many times since his first visit as a student in 1961. In 1972–3 he was Visiting Professor of American History at California State College, Dominguez Hills.

As well as writing occasional articles and book reviews, Daniel Snowman is also the author of *USA: The Twenties to Vietnam* (Batsford, 1968; published in the US by Harper & Row under the title *America Since 1920*); *Eleanor Roosevelt* (Edito-Service S.A., Geneva/Heron Books, 1970); *Kissing Cousins: An interpretation of British and American culture, 1945–1975* (Temple Smith, 1977; published in the US by New York UP/Harper & Row as *Britain and America: An interpretation of their culture, 1945–1975*); and *America Since 1920* (revised, updated edition, Heinemann Educational Books, 1978).

ROGER THOMPSON was born in 1933 and educated at St John's

College, Oxford. He taught at Eton College, 1957–67, did research at Harvard, 1967–69, and is now Reader in American History at the University of East Anglia, Norwich. His books include *The Golden Door* (Allman, London, 1969) and *Women in Stuart England and America* (Routledge, London and Boston, 1974); and he has edited *Samuel Pepys's Penny Merriments* (Constable/Columbia UP, 1976) and (with H. C. Allen), *Contrast and Connection* (Bell, London/Ohio State UP, 1976). He is working on puritan attitudes to sexuality in the seventeenth century, and was Visiting Professor at the University of Rhode Island, 1977–78.

ESMOND WRIGHT has been Director of the Institute of United States Studies and Professor of American History in the University of London since 1971. A graduate of Durham University and of the University of Virginia, he spent the war in the Middle East in Intelligence and Army Education and was demobilized as a Lieutenant-Colonel. From 1946–67 he was on the staff of Glasgow University and for 11 of those years he was Professor of Modern History. He resigned to become Conservative MP for the Pollok division of Glasgow. He was MP until his defeat in 1970.

He has written extensively on the American Revolution: *Washington and the American Revolution* (Penguin, 1973) and *Benjamin Franklin and American Independence* in *Men and Their Times* series (English Universities Press, 1966); *Fabric of Freedom 1763–1800* (Macmillan, 1964); *Causes and Consequences of the American Revolution* (Quadrangle Books, Chicago and the New York Times, 1966); and in 1974 he edited *A Tug of Loyalties* (Athlone Press), a series of essays on the Loyalists.

PETER CALVERT was educated at the Universities of Cambridge and Michigan, and is Reader in Politics at the University of Southampton. He is the author of *The Mexican Revolution, 1910–1914; the diplomacy of Anglo-American conflict* (Cambridge UP, 1968); *Latin America* (Macmillan/St Martin's Press,

NOTES ON THE CONTRIBUTORS

1969); *Revolution* (Key Concepts in Political Science) (Pall Mall & Macmillan/Praeger, 1970); *A Study of Revolution* (Clarendon Press, Oxford/Oxford UP, New York, 1970); *Mexico* (Nations of the Modern World) (Benn/Praeger, 1973); and *The Mexicans, how they live and work* (David & Charles/Praeger, 1975).

MAURICE PEARTON was educated at Oxford and the London School of Economics. After a career in the oil business in which he was particularly concerned with Eastern Europe, he switched to independent research, lecturing and writing. He is currently Visiting Fellow in the Centre of International Studies, Cambridge University. An occasional contributor to *The Economist, The American Review of East-West Trade*, and *Opera Canadia*, he has also contributed to BBC radio and presentations on Norwegian and Italian television, and is the author of *Oil and the Romanian State* (Clarendon Press, 1971); *The LSO at 70* (Gollancz, 1974); and co-author of *The International Trade in Arms* (Chatto & Windus/Praeger, 1972).

OWEN DUDLEY EDWARDS was born in Dublin in 1938 and educated at University College Dublin and the Johns Hopkins University. He has been lecturer in history at the University of Edinburgh since 1968, and has been visiting lecturer in history at the University of Oregon and at California State University at San Francisco, and visiting Associate Professor in History at the University of South Carolina.

He is co-editor of: *1916, The Easter Rising* (MacGibbon & Kee, 1968); *James Connolly: Selected Political Writings* (Cape/Grove Press, 1973); *Scotland, Europe and the American Revolution* (Students Publications Board, Edinburgh/St Martin's Press, 1976); and editor of *Conor Cruise O'Brien introduces Ireland* (Deutsch/McGraw-Hill 1969). He is the co-author of *Celtic Nationalism* (Routledge & Kegan Paul/ Barnes & Noble, 1968); and author of *The Sins of Our Fathers: Roots of Conflict in Northern Ireland* (Gill & Macmillan, Dublin, 1970); *The Mind of an Activist: James Connolly* (Gill & Macmillan, Dublin, 1971); *P. G. Wodehouse: A Critical and*

Historical Essay (Martin, Brian & O'Keeffe, London, 1977). He has written extensively for *The Irish Times, Tribune, The Scotsman,* and has reviewed for *The New York Times, Washington Post, The New Statesman, The Times Educational Supplement,* and various academic journals. A Scottish Nationalist, he is a frequent broadcaster on BBC and RTE.

HAROLD SHUKMAN was born and educated in London. He is a Fellow of St Antony's College and Lecturer in Modern Russian History at Oxford, and is the author of *Lenin and the Russian Revolution* (Batsford/Putnam's, 1967; Longman paperback 1977); *Lenin's Path to Power* (with George Katkov, Macdonald, 1971); and is General Editor of Longman's forthcoming multi-volume History of Russia. He is at present engaged on a history of the origins of Bolshevism.

LOUIS ALLEN was born in 1922. He is a military and ecclesiastical historian who teaches French literature at the University of Durham. A graduate of the Universities of Manchester, London and Paris, he served in British Intelligence in South-East Asia during the war, and has visited Japan several times since. He is the author of *Japan: The Years of Triumph* (Macdonald, 1971); *Sittang: The Last Battle* (Macdonald, 1973); *The End of the War in Asia* (Hart-Davis, 1976); *Singapore 1941–1942* (Davis-Poynter, 1977); and *John Henry Newman and the Abbé Jager* (Durham UP, 1976). He is a frequent broadcaster.

ROGER MORGAN was born in 1932, studied at the Universities of Cambridge, Paris and Hamburg, and was later a Research Associate at Harvard. He has been a lecturer at the Universities of London, Wales and Sussex, as well as holding several visiting professorships in the United States, and from 1968–74 was Deputy Director of Studies at the Royal Institute of International Affairs. He was Professor of European Politics at Loughborough University from 1975 to 1978, and became Head of the new European Centre for Studies in Democratic Politics in London in 1978. His books on German and international politics include *The German Social Democrats and the First International* (Cambridge UP, 1965); *The United States and West Germany* (Oxford UP, 1974); *West European Politics since 1945* (Batsford, 1973); and *The Unsettled Peace: A Study of the Cold War in Europe* (BBC publications, 1976).

PHILIP WINDSOR is Reader in International Relations at the London School of Economics. He was born in India in 1935 and educated at the University of Oxford and the Free University, Berlin. He worked for some years at the Institute for Strategic Studies in London, and then travelled for a while in Germany and Eastern Europe before joining the LSE. His publications include *Germany and the Management of Detente* (Chatto & Windus, London/Praeger, New York) and, with Adam Roberts, *Czechoslovakia 1968* (Chatto & Windus, London/Columbia UP, New York).

HAROLD BLAKEMORE took his Ph.D. in modern Chilean history at London University in 1955. Since 1965 he has been Secretary of the Institute of Latin American Studies at the University of London, and is also Reader in Latin American History. He has written, lectured and broadcast extensively on Chile in particular and Latin America in general, has visited the continent many times, and has been co-editor of the *Journal of Latin American Studies* since its inception in 1969, and a Corresponding Member of the Chilean Academy of History since 1970. The Spanish edition of his latest book, *British Nitrates and Chilean Politics, 1886–1896*, was published in Chile in 1977.